THE JUICE
DIET

THE JUICE DIET

• LOSE WEIGHT • DETOX • TONE UP • STAY SLIM & HEALTHY

CHRISTINE BAILEY

DUNCAN BAIRD PUBLISHERS

LONDON

The Juice Diet
Christine Bailey

Distributed in the USA and Canada by
Sterling Publishing Co., Inc.
387 Park Avenue South
New York, NY 10016-8810

This edition first published in the UK and USA in 2011 by
Duncan Baird Publishers, an imprint of
Watkins Publishing Limited
Sixth Floor, 75 Wells Street
London W1T 3QH

A member of Osprey Group

Managing Editor: Grace Cheetham
Editor: Judy Barratt
Managing Designer: Suzanne Tuhrim
Commissioned photography: Simon Smith and Toby Scott
Food Stylists: Mari Williams and Jennie Shapter

Bailey, Christine
 The juice diet : lose weight, detox, tone up, stay slim &
healthy / Christine Bailey.
    p. cm.
 Includes index.

1. Fruit juices--Therapeutic use. 2. Vegetable juices--
Therapeutic use. 3. Smoothies (Beverages)--Therapeutic
use. 4. Reducing diets. I. Title.
RM237.B35 2011
613.2'6--dc22
                    2010027167

ISBN 978-1-84483-964-3
10 9 8 7 6 5 4 3

Typeset in Univers
Color reproduction by Colourscan
Printed in China

For information about custom editions, special sales,
premium and corporate purchases, please contact Sterling
Special Sales Department at 800-805-5489 or specialsales@
sterlingpub.com.

Publisher's note
The information in this book is not intended as a substitute
for professional medical advice and treatment. The
information and recipes are unsuitable if you are pregnant
or lactating; are under the age of 18; are scheduled for or
have just had surgery; are diabetic or have metabolic
syndrome, Wilson's disease or AIDS; or suffer from any
eating disorder. If you have any special dietary
requirements or other medical conditions, it is
recommended that you consult a medical professional
before following any of the information or recipes
contained in this book. Watkins Publishing Limited, or any
other persons who have been involved in working on this
publication, cannot accept responsibility for any errors or
omissions, inadvertent or not, that may be found in the
recipes or text, nor for any problems that may arise as a
result of preparing one of these recipes or following the
advice contained in this work.

Notes on the recipes
Unless otherwise stated:
Use medium fruit and vegetables
Use fresh ingredients, including herbs and spices
1 tsp. = 5ml. 1 tbsp. = 15ml. 1 cup = 240ml.
The recipes in this book make one serving.

Author's acknowledgments
My thanks to everyone at DBP, especially Judy and Grace
for their ongoing support and advice with this book. Special
thanks to my wonderful, encouraging husband Chris and
my gorgeous boys, Nathan, Isaac and Simeon, who tried
every recipe and loved helping me with the juicing.

contents

introduction

If you want to feel slimmer, healthier and more alive, then the sensational Juice Diet is for you. Packed with 100 delicious recipes, this book shows you how easy it can be to shed the excess pounds and give your body a huge health boost at the same time. Whatever your health and weight loss goals, the Juice Diet has a perfect plan for you. Perhaps you want to fast-track your slimming program, in which case kickstart your weight loss with the Weekend Juice Blitz. If you're looking for something more steady and sustained, try the focused Juice Week, with its daily program of light meals and delicious juices that help shift excess weight in a mere seven days. If you're looking for a longer-term strategy, the Juice for Life program is the one for you. With juices that boost beauty, energy and immunity, too, there's no part of your physical well-being that's overlooked. The Juice Diet is 100 good-for-you juices that will have you feeling fabulous in no time at all.

why follow the juice diet?

Fresh juices are cleansing – their high water content helps hydrate your body and clear it of waste. They contain compounds, such as citric and malic acid, pectin and chlorophyll, which can absorb fats and toxins from your digestive tract. And all this can help you lose weight.

Juices also provide vitamins, minerals, phytonutrients and amino acids for optimal health. High in antioxidants, they protect against damaging free radicals and help improve liver function. Juices are also rich in enzymes to promote digestion and absorption of nutrients to create energy and support metabolism.

All the juices in this book have been carefully formulated to make sure you maximize your weight loss. The juices are powerhouses of nutrients that support and cleanse your body's systems and, most importantly, boost your metabolism, so that losing weight feels virtually effortless. Every recipe in this book has a nutrient analysis, telling you exactly how many calories and how much protein, carbohydrate and fat you consume when you drink the juice. These facts provide essential insight into all the good you're doing for your body. What's more, every one of the 100 juices in the book is

the benefits of the juice diet

Including fresh juices in your diet supercharges your body's ability to cleanse and heal and brings you the following amazing benefits. You'll:

• lose weight
• reduce cellulite and bloating
• improve digestion

• increase energy and vitality
• have a clearer, more radiant complexion, and healthier nails and hair
• suffer fewer infections, such as colds and flu
• lower your blood pressure
• have better mental clarity and focus

delicious, so whichever juices you drink and whichever plan you follow, you don't feel as though you're missing out at all.

How does the Juice Diet work? Apart from making sure your body has all the nutrients it needs for weight loss, the Juice Diet has been designed to support digestive and liver function in two primary ways specifically to promote weight loss. First, it cleans out your diet, reducing the amount of toxins your body is exposed to. Second, it provides nutrients that enable your digestive tract and liver to function optimally.

Your digestive tract processes the food you put into it and tries to clear out your system (mostly via your liver). Modern diets are often far removed from their natural state, so your food can lack the nutrients your digestive and liver systems need to work properly. As your body attempts to deal with waste, pollutants (toxins) build up inside you, straining your elimination system. This makes it harder to lose weight: if you can't detoxify, your body stores residual toxins in fat cells.

The more toxins in your system, the more fat cells your body needs to store them.

One important aid to weight loss is fiber: your digestive and elimination systems need fiber to keep moving the waste out of your body. Although juicing removes much of the fiber, I've devised my Juice Diet to include soluble fibres (such as psyllium husks, flaxseed, nuts and seeds) in the juices, and also plenty of whole-fruit smoothies. Quite simply, the Juice Diet works because it cleans out your system so you lose weight in the most natural way possible.

Losing weight and looking great Your activity and stress levels, your current weight, and how rigorously you stick to the diets will all affect how much weight you lose. And remember: looking great is not just about how much you weigh, but about being leaner, and feeling healthier and rejuvenated, too. These will show in your appearance, skin and hair and in your energy levels. The Juice Diet is about feeling slimmer and more alive, and transforming your health for good.

about the juice diet programs

This book is divided into five chapters that fall into two parts. The first part is devoted to three juice-diet programs: the Weekend Juice Blitz, the Juice Week and Juice for Life. These programs include juices and sample diet plans designed to help you lose weight. The second part of the book provides juices designed to promote healthy skin, hair and nails, supercharge your energy and vitality, and support your immune system. You can use these juices in combination with any of the diet programs, or you can use them during times when you aren't on a specific program to add variety and a burst of nutrients to your usual diet.

The Weekend Juice Blitz This is an intensive two-day juice fast that combines four juices daily with light, predominately raw snacks and meals to keep your metabolism high and enable you to lose weight fast. The juice recipes focus on using ingredients that help cleanse your body and replenish the nutrients you need for good digestion and optimum liver function.

The Juice Week This is a seven-day program of three or four juices and smoothies daily, along with light meals to speed up toxin removal and encourage weight loss. It includes juices to cleanse, as well as those to stabilize your blood sugar and reduce hunger and cravings.

Juice for Life This program shows you how to incorporate fresh, nutritious juices into your everyday life. The juices are particularly nourishing and many are substantial enough to provide a healthy breakfast or lunch, or energy snack.

How to use the programs Before you embark upon a juice program, use the questionnaire on the opposite page to guide you as to which program is most appropriate for your needs. Once you've done one program, feel free to move on to another. Periodically come back to the questionnaire to check your progress – perhaps every month or every three months. The important thing is to use the plans in a way that is achievable and sustainable for you.

the juice diet questionnaire

Use this questionnaire to work out which juice program is best for you. Answer yes or no.

- Are you struggling to lose weight?
- Do you suffer from bloating?
- Do you often have headaches or migraines?
- Do you regularly drink more than three servings of alcohol a week?
- Does even a little alcohol leave you lightheaded, nauseous or hungover?
- Do you have circles under your eyes?
- Do you suffer from excessive mucus, catarrh or sinus problems?
- Does your skin look dull, or do you suffer from acne or rashes?
- Do you have noticeable body odour or does your breath smell?
- Does your mouth taste bitter?
- Do you often feel a lack of energy?
- Do you have joint or muscle pains?
- Do you drink more than three cups of coffee or tea a day, and do they make you feel jittery?
- Do you frequently drink less than six glasses of water a day?
- Do you often eat processed or take-out foods?

What your score means

8 yeses or more: Weekend Juice Blitz Your score suggests your system is suffering from toxic overload. Weight loss won't come easily until you give your body a clean start. Begin with the Weekend Juice Blitz program and then, ideally, move on to the Juice Week to keep up the weight loss, or to the Juice for Life program to continue to nourish your liver and digestion and maintain your weight.

4–7 yeses: Juice Week You need to give some support to your body's cleansing mechanisms, so you're in peak condition to sustain any weight loss and feel slim. Following the Juice Week will maximize your nutrient intake and support your liver and digestion so that you can lose weight healthily. Once the week is over, maintain the healthier you by moving on to the Juice for Life program.

4 yeses or fewer: Juice for Life Keep up the good work! Your liver and digestion are doing a great job, but to maintain this include the cleansing, nourishing juices of the Juice for Life program in your daily diet.

getting started

All the juices in this book burst with nutrients and, for you to get the most from them, the rest of your diet and your lifestyle has to support their good work. Whichever program you follow, it's important to cut down on the foods and drinks that can adversely affect your body's ability to assimilate nutrients and to detoxify. You can also increase the weight-loss efficiency of the juices by taking some carefully chosen, natural supplements, as well as by including certain detoxifying treatments and by getting some gentle exercise.

KEY FOODS TO AVOID The foods to avoid are listed below. Many of them are common allergens or deplete your body of vital nutrients. Others upset blood-sugar levels, which can lead to cravings, or they may contain toxins that place a strain on your digestive system or liver. To help avoid any withdrawal symptoms or side effects (see page 15), begin cutting down on or removing these foods from your diet two or three days before you start your juice program. Then, if you're doing the Weekend Juice Blitz or the Juice Week, try to completely eradicate the following foods from your diet for the duration of the program. If you're following Juice for Life or the Beauty, Power or Immunity programs, try to reduce your consumption of them to a minimum. The foods to avoid are:

- gluten foods, such as wheat, barley, rye and spelt
- dairy foods, except for whey and low-fat plain yogurt, which are high in protein and low in lactose (a common allergen) so can usually be more easily tolerated.
- caffeine (including tea, coffee, chocolate, and energy and sports drinks)
- all carbonated soft drinks
- alcohol
- refined carbohydrates (sugary foods and drinks; pastries; white bread, rice and pasta; all processed foods and meals)
- trans and hydrogenated fats, which are found in deep-fried foods, processed fat spreads, some processed foods, and cookies, cakes and pastries (check labels if you're not sure)

- red meat and processed meat products, such as sausages, corned beef and burgers
- salt (especially look out for salt in processed foods, prepared foods, snacks, sauces, soups and so on – again, check the labels before you buy)

SUPERFOODS AND SUPPLEMENTS To support your weight loss and optimize your nourishment, there are some superfoods and supplements you can add to any of your juices. Some of these I've suggested in the juice recipes themselves, but you can add any of them to any recipe, according to your needs, if you like. Stock up on the following, all of which should be available from your local health-food store or good supermarket:

Seeds – pumpkin, sunflower, hemp, chia and flaxseed Seeds are packed with protein, fiber and essential fats, as well as minerals that are valuable for good liver function. Try to include at least one tablespoon of mixed seeds daily in one of your juices.

Psyllium This soluble fiber helps regulate bowel movements and provides food for the healthy bacteria (probiotics) in your gut. Take a teaspoon of psyllium in one of your juices or in a glass of water every day during your chosen juice program.

Probiotic powders Probiotics are the beneficial bacteria that live in your gut and they play a vital role in digestion, bolster immune health and generally help you lose weight. Find a probiotic powder that includes the strains *Lactobacillus acidophilus* and *Bifidobacteria*. Follow the product guidelines for dosage.

Glutamine powder Take a teaspoon of glutamine in a juice or a glass of water every night to help maintain the health of your gut lining and reduce the numbers of toxins entering your blood stream.

Superfood and antioxidant powders Wheatgrass, barley grass, spirulina, chlorella and berry powders provide your body with an extra nutrient shot. Add up to one teaspoon to each juice.

Milk thistle tincture Add this to your juices to support liver function and so encourage weight loss. Use the dosage recommended on the manufacturer's label.

Lecithin granules If you find it hard to digest fatty foods, a tablespoon of lecithin granules in one juice daily can help.

Fish oil Essential fats in fish oils produce hormone-like substances that control metabolism. Take a teaspoon daily either on its own or in a juice, or a tablespoon of flaxseed oil if you're vegetarian.

TREATMENTS For the Weekend Blitz and Juice Week, have one or two cleansing treatments every day to get the most out of the programs. If you're following Juice for Life, make time for at least one treatment twice a week. Here are some ideas to get you started.

Body brushing If you choose to practice only one treatment every day, make it this one. Body brushing stimulates your lymphatic system and improves your circulation. Use a long-handled, natural-bristle brush and brush in long strokes toward your heart. Avoid varicose or thread veins. Once you've finished brushing your body, have a warm shower.

Epsom salt bath Also known as magnesium sulfate crystals, Epsom salts provide your body with sulfur and magnesium, which are important for detoxification. Pour one or two cups into a warm bath and soak in it for 15 to 20 minutes. When you get out, put on warm nightclothes and go to bed. This will help elminiate toxins from your body.

Sauna and steam Heat encourages your body to sweat out impurities. Aim to sweat for 10 to 15 minutes, then have a cold shower, then return to the sauna or steam for another 15 minutes, then shower again. Drink plenty of water.

Massage This stimulates circulation and lymphatic drainage, and helps release emotional and physical tension. Massage can be expensive, but it does make a wonderful occasional treat during the longer weight-loss programs.

Relaxation Stress diverts energy away from digestion and detoxification, hampering weight loss. Try to make time every day for some relaxation – even if that's simply listening to your favorite piece of music without any distractions.

EXERCISE Brisk walking, cycling and swimming boost circulation and burn calories. If you're on the Weekend Juice Blitz, however, you may feel weak, so two daily walks of 15 minutes is enough. Aim for 30 minutes of brisk walking daily on the Juice Week. During Juice for Life, aim for at least two sessions of resistance or weight training and three or four 30-minute sessions of cardiovascular exercise every week.

TROUBLESHOOTING THE SIDE EFFECTS

After only a short time following the Juice Diet programs you're bound to feel great – slimmer and with lots more energy.

However, occasionally you may feel a few side effects during the first day or two. Often, side effects occur when toxins that have been stored in your body are released into your bloodstream to be processed by your liver. In general, the following side effects are nothing to worry about, will pass soon and are a clear sign that your Juice Diet is doing its work. Possible side effects are:

• withdrawal symptoms, such as headaches and cravings, as a result of cutting out certain foods and drinks
• noticeable body odour or bad breath
• changes in bowel movements, in particular diarrhea
• skin complaints (pimples or dry skin)
• fatigue or light-headedness

In order to minimize these side effects, drink filtered water regularly throughout each day (aim for at least six glasses). In addition, don't allow your blood-sugar levels to drop – include regular raw-food snacks and some protein snacks (such as a handful of nuts and seeds), too.

juicing basics

With the right equipment and preparation, juicing is not only simple to do, but easy to fit into a daily routine. To make the recipes in this book, you'll need a juicer, but also a blender – for the smoothies (which use whole fruit) and for when you want to add nutritional powders and supplements to your drinks.

Choosing a juicer The cheaper models of juicers tend to be "centrifugal" juicers, which means they grate the fruit and vegetables, then spin them rapidly to separate the juice from the pulp. If you have one of these, you'll need to juice in small batches and keep the juicer scrupulously clean, otherwise it will clog up easily. Centrifugal juicers are not suitable for tougher, fibrous vegetables, such as wheatgrass. The more expensive "masticating" juicers or "hydraulic juice presses" are more efficient at extracting juice and can handle a wider range of produce more effectively. Most importantly, though, whatever juicer you buy, make sure it is easy to clean and simple to put together.

Cleaning your juicer Always clean your juicer thoroughly immediately after juicing, otherwise it can become a breeding ground for bacteria. If you're making a day's worth of different juices, clean the juicer under running water between each batch to remove any excess pulp. Some vegetables and fruits can stain the juicer; if this happens, wash it with a solution of 1 teaspoon baking soda diluted in ½ cup water to help clean the stains more effectively.

Storing your juices To maximize the nutritional benefit of your juices, drink them as soon as you've made them. However, if you're making a large batch of one juice to drink through the day, pour it into a pitcher, cover it with an airtight lid or a sheet of plastic wrap, and store it in the refrigerator. Drink the whole batch on the same day, or freeze the remainder until you need it. You can add some lemon juice to help prevent discoloration.

Additional equipment As well as your juicer and blender, to make the juicing process as hassle-free as possible, ensure you have the following equipment:

- a hand-bristle brush for cleaning small parts of your juicer
- a citrus press
- weighing scales
- a cutting board, sharp knife and vegetable peeler
- a pitcher for storing juice
- plastic wrap to cover any stored juice

Choosing and preparing your ingredients
Choose produce that is ripe and ready to eat, but avoid any that is bruised or wilting. Making a juice from ripe foods maximizes the juice's nutrient levels and makes it easier for your body to digest. As much as possible choose organic produce. You can juice many organic fruits and vegetables without peeling them – this is great because you'll benefit from the significant portion of nutrients that lie just beneath the skin. Do wash all organic produce thoroughly to remove any dirt. If you're using non-organic produce, it's best to peel away the skin to reduce your exposure to any residue of chemical fertilizers and pesticides used during the growing process. If your juice includes fruits with a thick rind, such as citrus fruits, pineapples and melons, remove the rind before juicing, and always remove stems and large pits, as relevant.

Juicing uses a lot of produce, so it's worth buying in bulk every few days. If you have any excess fruits that you can't use before they become overripe, simply peel them, chop up the flesh and then freeze. You can add the chunks to smoothies to make iced drinks.

Extracting the juice For best results, alternate juicing a recipe's soft ingredients with those that are harder, as the hard foods will help push the softer ones through the juicer. Roll leafy green vegetables, such as spinach, into a ball and push the ball through the juicer with harder fruits or vegetables. Save very soft fruits, such as bananas and avocados, and overripe fruit for blending into smoothies.

the weekend juice blitz

Do you feel sluggish and tired? Do you need to kickstart your weight loss or detox after a period of overindulgence? If so, the Weekend Juice Blitz is for you. Designed to motivate you to start losing weight with the minimum effort, the Weekend Juice Blitz is packed with slimming, nourishing juices supercharged to clear out your system, improve digestion and aid weight loss.

In this chapter you'll find all the information you need to map out your juice weekend so it's blissfully stress-free. Not only is there a two-day planner, with suggested juices and meals for each day, but you'll also find a complete shopping list, so you can feel confident you have all the ingredients you need to follow my suggestions as easily as possible.

Whether you follow my two-day plan or choose your own juices for your blitz, feel assured that at the end of the two days you'll be well on a path to a noticeably slimmer, healthier, more vibrant you.

< beet and orange crush, page 38

the weekend juice blitz program

This program is a highly effective kickstart to a weight loss plan, but it's not intended as a long-term diet. To get the best results, read these preparation guidelines carefully and follow them as closely as you can.

Be prepared Before you do anything else, pick a date to start your Weekend Blitz. Write the date on your calendar to help make sure you stick to it. A long weekend is ideal for this program, so that you have a day to prepare and two days to blitz. On your preparation day avoid all meat protein and eat only light meals that include plenty of vegetables, fruit, fish and eggs. Steer completely clear of cream and cheese, but it's okay to have a little low-fat plain yogurt, if you like. Take special care to drink at least 6 glasses (52fl oz.) plain, filtered water and start cutting down on your coffee and tea consumption. At bedtime, take 1 tablespoon ground flaxseed in a large glass of water to kickstart the elmination of waste from your body.

Plan your juicing To make your Weekend Blitz as easy as possible, I've devised a shopping list (opposite) and complete menu (see pages 22–23) to guide you. However, if something I've suggested doesn't appeal to you, by all means substitute any of the other recipes in this chapter – just remember to adjust your shopping list accordingly and to keep the overall selection of juices varied. Also, it's important to ensure that you include at least one green juice daily to maximize your nutritional intake. All the recipes in the book make one serving.

Supplementary support I recommend that on both days of the Weekend Juice Blitz you supplement your juices and snacks with a multivitamin and mineral formula, an antioxidant or liver-support supplement and an omega-3 product (such as fish oil or flaxseed oil). Buy these in advance of starting the Blitz and choose the best-quality supplements you can afford. Your local health-food store should be able to advise you.

DRINKS

Bottled mineral water
Herbal teas – nettle,
  dandelion, fennel,
  chamomile, peppermint,
  valerian, lemon balm
Aloe vera juice

GROCERIES

Bag of ice cubes
Psyllium husks
Ground flaxseed
Flaxseed oil
Bag of mixed seeds
Shelled hemp
  seeds
Bean or nut pâté
Cashews
Almonds
Walnuts
Oat bran
Hummus
Small container of low-fat
  plain yogurt
Jar of marinated globe
  artichokes
Jar of olives
Can of mixed beans
  in water

Ingredients for 2 portions
  of homemade soup; or
  store-bought carton of
  low-sodium bean and
  vegetable soup
Miso soup sachets

Fruits

6 apples
3 pears
4 lemons
2 plums
1 pomegranate
8oz. seedless red grapes
2 oranges
1 mango
1 peach
1 pineapple
1 small watermelon
1 small cantaloupe melon
4oz. cherries

Vegetables

1 bag of curly kale
1 head of celery
1 head of romaine lettuce
1 raw beet
2 bags of mixed salad
1 bag of watercress

Sprouts
Cucumber
1 fennel bulb
2 carrots
1 small sweet potato
1 small piece of
  gingerroot

NON-FOOD

Milk thistle tincture
Antioxidant (berry)
  powder
Green superfood powder
  (or wheatgrass powder)
Supplements (see pages
  13–14)
Epsom bath salts

the weekend juice blitz rules

On each day of the program:

- avoid the foods listed on pages 12–13
- drink at least 6 glasses of water
- take 1 tbsp. ground flaxseed or 1–2 tsp. psyllium husks with a glass of water or a juice
- take 1 tbsp. ground mixed seeds

- drink four juices, one of them green
- include healthy snacks
- drink herbal teas
- get 15 minutes of gentle exercise in the morning and again in the afternoon
- use skin brushing in the morning and have an Epsom salt bath in the evening (see page 14)

the weekend juice blitz plan

day one

On waking A large cup of hot water with juice of ½ lemon

Breakfast Lemon Green Cleanser (page 24), then take supplements

Mid-morning A glass of water with milk thistle tincture (according to manufacturer's instructions); a large mug of chamomile tea; 2 tbsp. mixed pumpkin and sunflower seeds and 2 plums

Lunch Pomegranate Pick-Me-Up (page 30); a large bowl of mixed salad, including plenty of colorful vegetables, 1 handful of sprouts, 2 tbsp. shelled hemp seeds, and a dressing made by combining 2 tsp. flaxseed oil with 2 tsp. lemon juice

Mid-afternoon A cup of hot water with juice of ½ lemon or a cup of fennel tea; cucumber and celery crudités with 3 tbsp. hummus or nut pâté

Dinner Beet and Orange Crush (page 38). Bean and vegetable soup: Chop into chunks ½ red onion, 1 carrot, 1 celery stick, ½ sweet potato, ½ red bell pepper, and 1 tomato. In a saucepan, sauté the onion in ½ tsp.

olive oil, then add all the other ingredients. Pour in 1¼ cup low-salt vegetable stock, bring to a boil, then reduce the heat to low, cover with a lid and simmer for 10–15 minutes until all the vegetables are tender. Add 7oz. canned cannellini beans and heat through. Serve the soup chunky as it is or purée with a hand-held blender to make it smooth. Serve with 2 tbsp. pitted black olives and 4 marinated globe artichoke hearts

Evening Lettuce and Apple Sleepy Head **(page 43)**; 1 handful of almonds and 1 pear

Bedtime A large mug of lemon balm tea

day two

On waking A large cup of hot water with juice of ½ lemon

Breakfast Green Queen **(page 26)**, then take supplements

Mid-morning A glass of water with milk thistle tincture (according to manufacturer's instructions); a large cup of peppermint tea; 1 handful of walnuts and 1 apple

Lunch Pineapple Cleanse **(page 33)**; a

mug of miso soup (make according to package instructions) and a selection of raw vegetable sticks (such as carrot, celery and cucumber) with a small portion of hummus

Mid-afternoon A cup of hot water with juice of ½ lemon; a small bunch of red grapes and 1 tbsp. mixed seeds

Dinner Deep Root Cleanse **(page 39)**; a large bowl of mixed salad, including plenty of colorful vegetables, such as red and yellow bell peppers, cooked beets, carrot, celery or radish, topped with 7oz. canned mixed beans (drained) and 1 large handful of sprouts; a glass of water

Evening Cherry Melon **(page 43)**; 1 handful of cashews

Bedtime A large mug of valerian or chamomile tea

Coming off the Blitz On the first day following the Weekend Blitz, keep your meals light and simple. Thereafter, reintroduce excluded foods (such as meat and dairy) slowly so that you don't overload your system.

< lemon green cleanser

Kickstart your weight loss plan with this super-cleansing juice. Bursting with chlorophyll, potassium, pectin and vitamin C, this green cocktail will speed up your body's elimination of toxins to help blast that stubborn fat.

2 celery sticks • 3 large handfuls of kale leaves • 2 apples • 1 lemon, peeled • 1 tsp. green superfood powder (optional)

Juice all the food ingredients, then stir in the green superfood powder, if using.

HEALTH BENEFITS
*Kale is a super-green vegetable, perfect for supporting weight loss. It is a rich source of glucosinolates, which are **powerful detoxifiers**, and is also packed full with **potent anti-cancer phytochemicals**, including the sulfur compound sulforaphane.*

Nutritional analysis per serving: *Calories 124kcal • Protein 6.3g • Carbohydrates 19.6g [of which sugars 18.5g] • Fat 2.8g*

green queen

This is a delicious, peppery, cleansing juice, bursting with antioxidants and liver-protective phytonutrients to speed up elimination and help shift excess weight. The green superfood powder adds a nutrient boost for your energy levels.

2 celery sticks • 3½oz. cucumber • small bunch watercress • 2 pears • ½ tsp. green superfood powder

Juice all the food ingredients, then stir in the green superfood powder.

HEALTH BENEFITS
*Watercress and celery are **strong diuretics** that can help **tackle bloating**. Watercress is also **rich in vitamin B6** and other **liver-supportive** nutrients, to help **eliminate waste and carcinogens** from the body.*

Nutritional analysis per serving: *Calories 142kcal • Protein 2.9g • Carbohydrates 32.2g [of which sugars 30.5g] • Fat 0.8g*

ginger pear cooler >

Give your body a wake-up call with this cleansing, invigorating juice. Pear is a gentle laxative, aiding elimination, while a little gingerroot provides a kickstart for a sluggish digestive system. Cucumber will refresh and hydrate you.

½ lemon • 1in. piece of gingerroot, peeled • ½ cucumber, plus extra slice to decorate • 1 pear • ice cubes, to serve

Juice all the ingredients and serve over ice, decorated with a slice of cucumber.

HEALTH BENEFITS
*Rich in vitamin C, pectin, quercetin and limonene, the lemon in this juice is a highly **effective pick-me-up** that is **antioxidant, stimulates detoxification and digestion,** and may help **fight cancer cells**.*

Nutritional analysis per serving: *Calories 70kcal • Protein 1g • Carbohydrate 16.7g [of which sugars 16.5g] • Fat 0.2g*

citrus combo

This zesty combination provides plenty of immunity-boosting vitamin C to keep you fit for the Weekend Blitz. When you peel citrus fruits for juicing, try to leave the pith on as it contains pectin, which can help absorb fats and toxins from your digestive tract. As a result, this combo is an all-round fantastic slimming aid.

1 pink grapefruit, peeled • 1 small lemon, peeled • 1 orange, peeled • 2 carrots

Juice all the ingredients.

HEALTH BENEFITS
*Pink grapefruit is a good source of **cancer-protective lycopene**. Bioflavonoids in citrus pith are **powerful antioxidants** that **strengthen the capillaries, enhance skin condition** and generally promote **optimal health**.*

Nutritional analysis per serving: *Calories 141kcal • Protein 3.8g • Carbohydrate 31.7g [of which sugars 29.8g] • Fat 0.7g*

crimson cabbage

Like coleslaw in a glass, this juice combination is packed full of vitamins, minerals and fiber. The red grapes provide an instant energy lift, while the fiber from the flaxseed helps stabilize blood-sugar levels and curb sugar cravings to keep your diet on track.

5½oz. red cabbage • ⅓ cup seedless red grapes • 2 apples • 1 carrot • ½ tsp. ground flaxseed • ice cubes, to serve

Juice all the ingredients and serve over ice.

HEALTH BENEFITS

*Cabbage contains a range of **powerful sulfurous chemicals** that **protect the liver** and enhance elimination. Red cabbage contains the most **anthocyanidins**, potent antioxidants with **anti-cancer, anti-microbial and anti-inflammatory properties**.*

Nutritional analysis per serving: *Calories 144kcal • Protein 2.7g • Carbohydrates 33.8g [of which sugars 32.4g] • Fat 0.8g*

fennel enzyme boost

A essential aid to any weight loss program, this juice combines celery, which helps the body eliminate excess fluid, and super-slimming fennel, which stimulates your gall bladder and increases your flow of bile to help break down your body's fat.

2 oranges, peeled • 1 fennel bulb • 1 handful of alfalfa sprouts • 2 celery sticks • 1 slice of orange and a little grated zest, to serve

Juice all the ingredients. Serve decorated with a slice of orange and sprinkled with a little orange zest.

HEALTH BENEFITS
*Rich in **enzymes and fiber**, alfalfa sprouts are easy to digest and can help break food down. They are packed with **cleansing chlorophyll** to **support toxin removal**, and plenty of **antioxidants** to support the liver and **protect against degenerative diseases**. They are also rich in **B-vitamins** to help **support energy production**.*

Nutritional analysis per serving: *Calories 131kcal • Protein 6.1g • Carbohydrates 26.2g [of which sugars 23.8g] • Fat 1g*

pomegranate pick-me-up >

This juice is a wonderful energizer, thanks to the natural sugars in the grapes, pomegranate and apple. Yogurt provides protein that, together with the flaxseed, helps stabilize blood sugar to stave off hunger.

1 pomegranate, seeds and flesh • ²/₃ cup seedless red grapes • 1 apple • 5 tbsp. soy yogurt • 1 tsp. antioxidant berry powder (optional) • 1 tsp. ground flaxseed

Juice the fruits, then pour the juice into a blender, add the rest of the ingredients and process until smooth.

HEALTH BENEFITS
*Pomegranates are **packed with antioxidants**, including **polyphenols and bioflavonoids**, to **strengthen immunity**. These nutrients also help **strengthen collagen in the skin and capillaries**, helping to **tackle cellulite**. Pomegranate seeds are rich in the antioxidant vitamin E.*

Nutritional analysis per serving: *Calories 213kcal • Protein 4.2g • Carbohydrates 47.6g [of which sugars 44g] • Fat 2g*

< pineapple cleanse

If you're feeling a bit sluggish, try this cleansing and healing combo. Fennel contains essential oils such as anethole, which are mildly diuretic and help the body get rid of excess fluid to make you feel instantly lighter. Pineapple, aloe vera and ginger are well-known digestive aids.

½ pineapple, peeled • 2 apples • 1 fennel bulb • 1in. piece of gingerroot, peeled • 1 tsp. aloe vera juice • ice cubes, to serve

Juice the pineapple, apples, fennel and ginger. Pour the juice into a blender, add the aloe vera and process to combine. Serve over ice.

HEALTH BENEFITS
*Pineapple contains the **healing enzyme bromelain**, which helps **break down protein, reduce inflammation and aid digestion**. Pineapples are rich in **beta-carotene and vitamin C**, two of the many **antioxidants that protect the body** from free-radical damage, plus **vitamin B1**, which we need for **energy production**. Aloe vera is **antibacterial and antifungal**, and so helps to support your immune system, and has **strong detoxifying properties**.*

Nutritional analysis per serving: *Calories 126kcal • Protein 2g • Carbohydrates 29.3g [of which sugars 28.4g] • Fat 0.7g*

guava and kiwi tonic

This is a hydrating juice that gets its creamy texture from the tropical guava. Rich in soluble fiber, guava can promote weight loss because it helps you feel fuller for longer. A teaspoon of green superfood powder gives a superboost to the cleansing power of this juice.

½ cucumber • 2 kiwifruits, peeled • 1 guava, peeled • 1 tsp. green superfood powder

Juice the food ingredients, then pour into a blender, add the green superfood powder and process to combine.

HEALTH BENEFITS
Guavas are an excellent source of the antioxidants **vitamins A, C and E, and beta-carotene and lycopene**. *They are also rich in* **potassium** *to maintain* **healthy blood pressure**. *Both kiwifruits and guavas are packed with* **vitamin C** *to* **boost energy**, *and to* **support your adrenals** *if you're feeling stressed.*

Nutritional analysis per serving: *Calories 90kcal • Protein 2.9g • Carbohydrates 18.1g [of which sugars 16.6g] • Fat 1.1g*

watermelon reviver >

Watermelon is the perfect low-calorie fruit for the Weekend Blitz, and it has wonderful cleansing properties, too. Adding cinnamon and ground flaxseed to the juice helps stabilize blood-sugar levels to prevent mid-afternoon energy slumps and to stave off any cravings.

4½oz. watermelon, peeled • 5½oz. strawberries • 1 tsp. ground flaxseed • a pinch of cinnamon

Juice the watermelon and strawberries, then stir in the flaxseed and cinnamon.

HEALTH BENEFITS
Watermelon is rich in **immunity-boosting beta-carotene**. *Include the seeds when juicing, since they are packed full of* **protective vitamin E**.

Nutritional analysis per serving: *Calories 106kcal • Protein 2.8g • Carbohydrates 19.4g*

< berry cream blitz

This satisfying juice keeps hunger pangs at bay. Rich in protein and essential fats, it provides a super-dose of nutrients to support your metabolism. The pectin in the berries helps stimulate digestion, while flaxseed oil boosts your intake of essential fats to aid weight loss.

½ lemon, peeled • 1⅓ cup seedless red grapes or scant ⅔ cup red grape juice • 1½ cups frozen mixed berries • 1 tsp. tahini • 1 tsp. flaxseed oil

Juice the lemon and grapes. Pour the juice into a blender, add the remaining ingredients and ½ cup water and process until smooth.

HEALTH BENEFITS
*Tahini is made from sesame seeds and provides plenty of **calcium, magnesium, zinc, selenium and vitamin E**, which all support detoxification. The berries and grapes are packed with **antioxidants** to **fight damaging free radicals** in your body.*

Nutritional analysis per serving: *Calories 259kcal • Protein 5.7g • Carbohydrates 49.8g [of which sugars 45.9g] • Fat 5.9g*

instant spring clean

An instant detoxifier, this juice will counter times of overindulgence and give your weight loss plan a great boost. The combination of apples and vegetables rids your body of excess fluid and waste products to put the spring back in your step.

1 handful of flat-leaf parsley • 5½oz. celeriac, peeled • 2 apples • ½in. piece horseradish or 1 radish • 2 celery sticks • 1 handful of ice cubes

Juice all the ingredients except the ice. Pour the juice into a blender, add the ice and process until smooth.

HEALTH BENEFITS
*Adding horseradish or radish to this juice **stimulates your digestion** and the **production of bile** from the gall bladder. This helps **break down fats**, making this juice a powerful cleanser and weight loss aid.*

Nutritional analysis per serving: *Calories 98kcal • Protein 2.9g • Carbohydrates 20.3g [of which sugars 19g] • Fat 0.9g*

beet and orange crush

Beets and orange is a classic flavor combination and this delicious juice is the perfect pick-me-up for when your energy levels are low. Blending in mango and psyllium increases the fiber content of the drink, which boosts the juice's cleansing power.

1 raw beet • 2 oranges, plus extra peel to decorate • 1¾oz. mango flesh • ½ tsp. psyllium husks

Juice the beet and orange. Pour the juice into a blender, add the mango and psyllium and process until smooth. Serve decorated with a twist of orange peel.

HEALTH BENEFITS
*Beet's natural sugars make its juice rich in **instant energy** to stop you from feeling tired. It can help maintain **healthy blood** and is a **great internal cleanser**, because its **antioxidants**, including betacyanin, can help **stimulate detoxification enzymes** in the liver. Beets have been shown to help **lower cholesterol and increase the production of bile**, which your body needs to **emulsify fats**.*

Nutritional analysis per serving: *Calories 139kcal • Protein 4g • Carbohydrates 32g [of which sugars 30g] • Fat 0.4g*

deep root cleanse

This sweet-tasting, cleansing juice will help you feel instantly lighter and healthier. The sweet potato provides complex carbohydrates to boost your energy levels, while the natural sugars in the juice will help satisfy any sweet cravings you might have.

2 small carrots • ½ sweet potato • 2 apples • ½ cucumber

Juice all the ingredients.

HEALTH BENEFITS
*Carrots are loaded with **protective carotenoids** that support **eye and skin health**. Carrot juice is easy to digest and very **soothing for the digestive tract**. Sweet potato is rich in **B-vitamins**, which help **raise spirits**, as well as the antioxidant **vitamins A and C**, which help **protect your body against disease**, and **fiber to keep your bowels healthy**.*

Nutritional analysis per serving: *Calories 191kcal • Protein 3.1g • Carbohydrates 45.5g [of which sugars 27.9g] • Fat 0.8g*

digestive aid

This light, sweet juice is packed with super-nutrients to cleanse, heal and support the digestive process. The enzymes in pineapple help break down proteins in food, while the cleansing apple promotes elimination.

8oz. pineapple, peeled • 1 apple • 1 celery stick • 1 handful of mint leaves • 1 tsp. green superfood powder • 1 tsp. probiotic powder (optional) • ice cubes, to serve

Juice all the food ingredients. Pour the juice into a blender, add the powders and process to combine. Serve over ice.

HEALTH BENEFITS
*Mint **soothes the digestive tract** and is particularly useful for **relieving flatulence and indigestion** and **easing muscle spasms**. Adding a spoonful of probiotic powder to the juice **boosts levels of beneficial bacteria** to help process food and **support optimal health**.*

Nutritional analysis per serving: *Calories 68kcal • Protein 0.8g • Carbohydrates 16.7g [of which sugars 16.1g] • Fat 0.3g*

perfect passion >

Divine, sweet-tasting nectar, this juice combines energizing tropical fruits with cleansing carrot. Diluting the juice with sparkling water and topping it with ice cubes turns it into a wonderfully refreshing drink.

1 lime, peeled • 1 papaya, seeded and peeled • 3 carrots, plus extra to decorate • 2 passion fruit, flesh and seeds • 1 tsp. probiotic powder • sparkling water, to taste (optional)

Juice the lime, papaya and carrots. Pour the juice into a blender, add the passion fruit and probiotic powder and process briefly to combine. Dilute with sparkling water, if using, and decorate with a little grated carrot.

HEALTH BENEFITS
*Bursting with **vitamin C and antioxidants**, including **eye-protective carotenoids, and lutein and zeaxanthin**, papaya is a nourishing superfood. It is a perfect **digestive aid**, too, **rich in enzymes such as papain**, which help **break down protein** and **cleanse the digestive tract**.*

Nutritional analysis per serving: *Calories 89kcal • Protein 2.9g • Carbohydrates 18.4g [of which sugars 9.4g] • Fat 0.6g*

< lettuce and apple sleepy head

This is a perfect drink for the day's end, since lettuce contains soporific compounds which help induce sleep. Best sipped after dinner, the juice also contains pectin (from the apples) and digestive enzymes (from the pineapple) that help eliminate toxins that have built up during the day.

1 apple, plus extra to decorate • 4oz. romaine lettuce • 4½oz. pineapple, peeled

Juice all the ingredients. Dilute with water, if desired, and serve decorated with a slice of apple.

HEALTH BENEFITS
*Water-rich romaine lettuce is wonderfully hydrating. It bursts with antioxidants, including **carotenoids and vitamin C**, as well as **fiber and folate**, making it a great **heart-healthy** vegetable that helps **prevent the oxidation of cholesterol** and **reduce levels of damaging homocysteine**. Its **high potassium** content can help **keep blood pressure at a healthy level**.*

Nutritional analysis per serving: *Calories 97kcal • Protein 1.8g • Carbohydrates 21.9 [of which sugars 20.6g] • Fat 1g*

cherry melon

This cleansing juice provides plenty of antioxidants to support the body's detoxification, tackle cellulite and boost vitality. Melon seeds are rich in the antioxidants zinc, selenium and vitamin E, so juice them with the flesh, or munch on them separately.

4oz. watermelon, peeled, plus extra to decorate • 4oz. cantaloupe melon, peeled • 4oz. cherries, pitted, plus extra to decorate • ice cubes, to serve

Juice all the ingredients. Serve the juice over ice, topped with a watermelon wedge or cherries.

HEALTH BENEFITS
*Rich in **anthocyanins and quercetin**, cherries are strongly **anti-inflammatory and support immune health**. Cherries can also help you **unwind and destress**, since they are a great source of **melatonin**, a nutrient that's important for **promoting sleep**.*

Nutritional analysis per serving: *Calories 118kcal • Protein 2.2g • Carbohydrates 27.8g [of which sugars 27.5g] • Fat 0.6g*

the juice week

This seven-day juice plan is the road to a slimmer and healthier you. Whether you're looking to get rid of stubborn fat, develop a leaner, cleaner body, or supercharge your energy, a week of cleansing, fresh juices is a sure way to see results. The cleanse to your digestive system and liver function should quickly rejuvenate you; and by the end of the week, you should have started to see a visible reduction in excess weight.

To get you started I've devised a day-by-day plan for you to follow. Every day, I've suggested a series of mouthwatering juices that are packed with essential vitamins and phytonutrients that support your metabolism, nourishment and vitality, and meal suggestions and herbal teas to support your health. The aim is to optimize your nutritional intake, minimize cravings and hunger pangs, and eliminate foods that are disruptive to your body's metabolism. Follow the plan and in only one week see a leaner, healthier-looking you.

< mulled fruit reviver, page 65

the juice week program

All the juices in the Juice Week are low in calories and high in metabolism-boosting nutrients. Cleansing, energizing and fat-busting, these juices will get your body in peak condition in days.

The juice and food guidelines in the Juice Week offer around 1,100 to 1,200 calories a day, to give effective and healthy weight loss. Every day, the juices in the plan provide your body with a powerhouse of nutrients to nourish and enhance all its systems as you lose weight. Once you've finished the Juice Week, move on to the Juice for Life program, in which you gradually increase calories to more sustainable levels, while keeping at least one freshly made juice in your diet daily.

Following the Juice Week program

Choose a week that you can devote fully to the plan – one that's as clear from commitments as possible. I recommend you start the Juice Week on a Saturday, or other non-working day. This will help you adjust to the new way of eating while you're able to chill out at home. As with the Weekend Blitz, you need to give yourself time in advance to prepare and

stock up on ingredients and supplements. Make a shopping list of all the ingredients you need for the week and buy them in advance. Follow the guidelines on page 20 to help prepare your body before the week. The night before you start the program, take 1 tbsp. of ground flaxseed in a large glass of warm water to kickstart the cleansing process.

Using the seven-day program I've devised for you should make the diet easier to follow, but by all means change the juice recipes if you see a juice that doesn't appeal or if you're intolerant to any of the ingredients. You can substitute in any of the other juice recipes in this chapter. Make sure you drink a wide range of colorful juices each day to maximize your nutrients. Finally, for best results, follow the Juice Week rules set out opposite. These are intended to make the plan easier to follow while maximizing its effectiveness.

the juice week rules

Follow the Weekend Juice Blitz rules set out on page 22. In addition, on each day of this program:

- take the supplements suggested on pages 13–14
- drink three juices – select from the juices in this chapter (if you're not following the plan, which uses them anyway) and choose a range of colorful juices, ensuring that at least one of them is a green juice
- eat at least one colorful, leafy green salad
- have a serving of cruciferous vegetables (broccoli, cauliflower, kale, cabbage, Brussels sprouts, and so on) in a juice, soup or salad
- include protein foods throughout the day – these will help to stabilize your blood-sugar levels. Protein foods can include nuts, seeds, beans, legumes, fish, eggs and soy or live plain yogurt
- drink herbal teas, green tea or miso soup if you feel that you need a warming drink
- use skin brushing in the morning and have an Epsom salt bath in the evening (see page 14)
- take a 30-minute brisk walk that leaves you slightly breathless (alternatively, you could try cycling or swimming if you prefer)

Coming off the diet

Once you come to the end of the seven-day program, try not to be tempted to go back to your old ways. The few days after the week program can be a difficult time in which your body needs to readjust to a more normal way of eating. Try to reintroduce excluded foods and drinks slowly. During this time monitor whether or not you suffer any adverse reactions to any of the foods you've kept out of your diet.

In general, as you come off the Juice Week program, keep your meals light and continue to include raw foods, juices and smoothies daily for as long as you can. Follow the guidelines in the Juice for Life chapter to further boost your health and weight loss in the long term.

the juice week plan: days 1–4

day one

On waking A glass of hot water with juice of ½ lemon, or a cup of green tea

Breakfast Green Machine **(page 52)**; a bowl of mixed berries with 3 tbsp. plain yogurt and 2 tbsp. mixed seeds

Mid-morning snack 1 handful of Brazil nuts; a cup of nettle or green tea

Lunch Gazpacho Smoothie **(page 61)**; Leafy green mixed salad: Mix together 1 large handful of mixed greens (watercress, arugula, mâche and baby spinach) and chopped ½ red bell pepper, 1 celery stick, ¼ cucumber and 2 tomatoes. Drain 7oz. canned lima beans and toss into the salad. Sprinkle with 1 handful of alfalfa sprouts

Mid-afternoon snack 3 tbsp. hummus with celery, cucumber and carrot sticks; a cup of hot water with juice of ½ lemon

Early evening Ruby Crush **(page 72)**

Dinner Steamed salmon fillet: Sprinkle 1 tbsp. lemon juice and a little chopped dill over 1 salmon fillet and steam for 15 minutes until cooked through. Serve with a large plate of mixed, stir-fried vegetables sprinkled with 1 tsp. sesame seeds; a cup of chamomile or fennel tea

day two

On waking A glass of hot water with juice of ½ lemon, or a cup of green tea

Breakfast Breakfast Booster **(page 55)**

Mid-morning snack Celery and cucumber sticks with 2 tbsp. olive tapenade or nut butter; a cup of peppermint tea

Lunch Parsley Pleaser **(page 62)**; Curried lentil soup: In a little olive oil sauté ½ chopped red onion with ½ tsp. turmeric and ½ tsp. grated gingerroot. Add 3 tbsp. red lentils and 5½oz. grated carrot and generous 1 cup vegetable stock. Bring to a boil, then reduce the heat to low and simmer, covered, for 15–20 minutes until the lentils are tender. Remove from the heat, add a little soy milk to taste and purée until smooth. 2 plums

Mid-afternoon snack 1 handful of almonds and a cup of hot water with juice of ½ lemon

Early evening Lean Lychee **(page 73)**

Dinner Roasted vegetables with tofu: Preheat the oven to 350°F. Cut into chunks ½ red and 1½ orange bell peppers and ½ red onion. Put into a roasting pan with 1 sliced zucchini and 4½oz. cubed firm tofu and drizzle with a little olive oil and tamari and roast for 25–30 minutes until soft. Add 4 halved cherry tomatoes and roast for 10 minutes more; serve with a green salad. A cup of chamomile or fennel tea

day three

On waking A cup of hot water with juice of ½ lemon

Breakfast Liver Support **(page 56)**; 1 poached egg and 2 broiled tomatoes

Mid-morning snack 3 prunes and 1 tbsp. pumpkin seeds; a cup of nettle or dandelion tea

Lunch Mango No-Tox **(page 64)**; a large mixed salad: Mix 1 large handful each of spinach leaves and watercress and add some cherry tomatoes and colorful vegetables, such as red bell pepper, radish and celery. Serve with 2 broiled fresh

sardines or 3½oz. canned sardines in spring water

Mid-afternoon snack Sticks of celery, cucumber and carrot; a cup of green tea

Early evening Lemon Refresher **(page 74)**

Dinner Vegetable and bean stew: Chop ½ red onion and 1 garlic clove and sauté in a saucepan until soft. Slice ¼ red bell pepper, 1 zucchini and ½ leek and add to the pan with 7oz. canned chopped tomatoes, 7oz. chickpeas or kidney beans and scant 1 cup vegetable stock. Bring to a boil, then reduce the heat to low, cover and simmer for 10 minutes until the vegetables are tender. Stir in 1 handful of spinach leaves just before serving. 1 handful of red grapes; a cup of lemon balm tea

day four

On waking A cup of hot water with juice of ½ lemon

Breakfast Double Plum Shake **(page 56)**

Mid-morning snack A cup of miso soup and 2 tbsp. mixed seeds

Lunch Mulled Fruit Reviver **(page 65)**;

2 eggs, scrambled with 1 handful of baby spinach leaves and 2 sliced mushrooms; a cup of green tea

Mid-afternoon snack 1 pear and 1 handful of almonds; a cup of hot water with juice of ½ lemon

Early evening Minted Greens **(page 75)**

Dinner Steamed Asian chicken: Steam a skinless chicken breast with a splash of soy sauce, ½ tsp. grated gingerroot, 1 crushed garlic clove, a pinch of red chili flakes, 2 chopped scallions and a few drops of sesame oil, for 30 minutes until cooked through. Serve with 1 handful of watercress and 7oz. prepared vegetables; a cup of chamomile tea

day five

On waking A cup of hot water with juice of ½ lemon

Breakfast Sunrise Delight **(page 58)**; ½ cup low-fat plain yogurt with 2 tbsp. mixed seeds

Mid-morning snack 4 cherry tomatoes and 1 handful of walnuts

Lunch Lima bean and vegetable soup: Chop and sauté ½ onion, 1 leek, ½ fennel bulb, 1 celery stick and 1 garlic clove in a saucepan for 4–5 minutes to soften. Add scant 1¼ cups vegetable stock and bring to a boil; reduce the heat to low and simmer, covered, for 15 minutes, until tender. Drain 7oz. canned lima beans, add to the pan and heat through. Purée until smooth. Season. 1 nectarine; a cup of hot water and lemon juice

Mid-afternoon snack Cucumber Cleanser **(page 66)**; 1 handful of olives

Early evening Stress Tonic **(page 76)**

Dinner Tomato and mushroom omelet: Beat 2 eggs; stir in 1 chopped tomato and 2 sliced mushrooms. Cook over high heat until only a little liquid is left on top; flip over to finish off for 1–2 minutes. Serve with green salad with juice of ½ lemon, a little olive oil and black pepper; a cup of green tea

day six

On waking A cup of hot water with juice of ½ lemon

Breakfast Carrot Blast **(page 58)**; a bowl of berries with 2 tbsp. chopped nuts

Mid-morning snack 1 apple and

1 handful of pumpkin seeds; a cup of lemon and ginger tea

Lunch Sweet Fennel **(page 68)**; Bean and artichoke salad: Mix together 1 handful of spinach leaves and watercress and 1 handful of pitted black olives. Slice ½ red onion, drain 5½oz. canned chickpeas, and chop 4 marinated artichokes and ½ red bell pepper, and mix in. Dress with juice of ½ lemon and 1 tbsp. olive oil.

Mid-afternoon snack 2 oat cakes spread with nut butter

Early evening Raspberry Twist **(page 78)**

Dinner Baked trout: Preheat the oven to 350°F. Roast quartered ½ red bell pepper, 4½oz. cubed butternut squash and ½ red onion, sliced into chunks, in olive oil for 15 minutes. Stir in 1 large handful of snow peas. Top with a boneless trout fillet and a little olive oil. Bake for 10 minutes until cooked through. Season. Serve with a salad; a cup of peppermint tea

day seven

On waking A glass of hot water with juice of ½ lemon

Breakfast Chlorophyll Wonder **(page 60)**; muesli of 1 tbsp. each of millet and quinoa flakes, and 2 tbsp. buckwheat flakes, 2 tbsp. mixed seeds, 1 tbsp. chopped nuts and 1 handful of raisins. Serve with soy milk or plain yogurt

Mid-morning snack A bunch of red grapes and 1 handful of pecans

Lunch Cherry Healer **(page 71)**; curried lentil soup (see Day 2); 1 handful of walnuts

Mid-afternoon snack 3 tbsp. hummus and 1 handful of carrot sticks

Early evening Chili Tomato **(page 79)**

Dinner 2 eggs, scrambled with 1 slice smoked salmon; Mixed salad: Mix together 1 large handful of mixed greens (such as watercress, arugula, mâche or other green leaves), a grated small carrot and 2 tbsp. alfalfa sprouts. Cook 1 small beet and chop, and then combine with chopped ½ red bell pepper and chopped ½ avocado. Dress with juice of ½ lemon and 1 tbsp. flaxseed or olive oil; a cup of lemon and ginger tea

green machine >

This combination of sweet and savory juices creates a great liver and digestive tonic and is a great way to boost your intake of greens. The bromelain in the pineapple aids your digestion, while broccoli helps stimulate your liver function to keep your body toxin-free.

9oz. pineapple, peeled, plus extra slice to decorate • 4 broccoli florets • 2 celery sticks • 1 tsp. green superfood powder • ice cubes, to serve

Juice all the food ingredients, then stir in the green superfood powder. Serve over ice, decorated with a slice of pineapple.

HEALTH BENEFITS
Broccoli is rich in **vitamin C***, as well as other* **antioxidants***, and sulfurous compounds known as* **glucosinolates***, which are* **powerful aids to detoxification***. They include sulforaphane and indole-3-carbinol, which have been found to be* **anti-cancerous, particularly against breast cancer***. Broccoli also provides plenty of* **soluble fiber to support bowel health***.*

Nutritional analysis per serving: *Calories 121kcal • Protein 3.1g • Carbohydrates 26.6g [of which sugars 25.6g] • Fat 1g*

< breakfast booster

Kickstart your day! Adding a scoop of protein powder to this energizing juice helps keep your blood sugar balanced and provides fuel for your liver. Parsley is diuretic so helps tackle fluid retention, while melons are hydrating and cleansing, making them ideal for a weight loss diet.

5½oz. cantaloupe melon, peeled • 1 small lemon, peeled • 1 handful of flat-leaf parsley • ½ mango, peeled, pitted and chopped • 1½ tbsp. vanilla whey protein powder • 1 tsp. ground flaxseed

Juice the melon, lemon and parsley. Pour the juice into a blender and add the remaining ingredients. Blend until smooth.

HEALTH BENEFITS
*The orange-fleshed cantaloupe melon provides plenty of **beta-carotene and vitamin C** to **support immune health**, while its **high potassium** content **helps lower blood pressure and tackle fluid retention**.*

Nutritional analysis per serving: *Calories 197kcal • Protein 23g • Carbohydrates 21.1g [of which sugars 17.1g] • Fat 3.1g*

liver support

Since eliminating waste and toxins efficiently is an important aid to weight loss, supporting the work of the liver is crucial in any diet. This delicious green juice is packed full with liver-supportive nutrients and digestive enzymes to speed up waste removal and help blast the fat.

4 asparagus spears • 2 broccoli florets • 5½oz. pineapple, peeled • ½ cucumber • a few drops milk thistle tincture

Juice all the ingredients, then stir well to mix.

HEALTH BENEFITS
Asparagus contains a natural chemical called **asparagine** *and* **high levels of potassium,** *which together* **reduce fluid retention and support liver and kidney health.** *This vegetable also contains organic compounds called* **glucosinolates** *to promote* **detoxification.**

Nutritional analysis per serving: *Calories 91kcal • Protein 3.5g • Carbohydrates 18.3g [of which sugars 17.2g] • Fat 0.8g*

double plum shake >

This smoothie provides a satisfying mid-morning snack. It can both support digestion and cleanse, while providing plenty of protein to sustain your energy levels. The combination of beneficial bacteria (in the soy yogurt), fiber and antioxidants provides optimum nourishment for your bowel.

3 red plums, halved and pitted, plus extra slice to decorate • 2 prunes, pitted • 5 tbsp. soy yogurt • ½ cup soy milk • 1 tsp. flaxseed oil • 1 tsp. ground flaxseed

Put all the ingredients into a blender and process until smooth and creamy. Serve decorated with a plum slice.

HEALTH BENEFITS
Fresh plums and prunes (dried plums) contain **immunity-boosting phytonutrients.** *Prunes are high in* **fiber,** *giving them a* **mild laxative** *effect, aiding bowel function. Like other dried fruit, prunes* **boost energy** *and provide* **potassium** *to* **support fluid balance** *in the body.*

Nutritional analysis per serving: *Calories 201kcal • Protein 10.5g • Carbohydrates 26.4g [of which sugars 22.2g] • Fat 7.2g*

sunrise delight

A sweet juice with plenty of protein to keep your blood-sugar levels balanced through the morning, Sunrise Delight is also packed with instant-energy fruits to kickstart the day. Adding a little cinnamon also helps stabilize blood sugar to beat cravings and so boost weight loss.

2 apricots, pitted • 2 oranges, peeled • 1 lemon, peeled • 2¼oz. silken tofu • ice cubes, to serve (optional) • ½ tsp. cinnamon, to serve

Juice all the fruits, then pour the juice into a blender and add the tofu; process until smooth. Serve over ice, if using, and sprinkle with the cinnamon.

HEALTH BENEFITS
*Apricots are rich in **vitamin C and beta-carotene** that help protect **against eye problems and cancer**, as well as neutralizing damaging free radicals. They are rich in **soluble fiber**, so help **lower cholesterol** and **remove toxins**.*

Nutritional analysis per serving: *Calories 166kcal • Protein 8.8g • Carbohydrates 27.9g [of which sugars 26.3g] • Fat 3.1g*

carrot blast >

Creamy and satisfying, this low-carb drink provides instant energy to keep you going between meals. The addition of almonds and soy milk provides plenty of protein, minerals and unsaturated fat to give your body a really nutritious blast.

2 carrots • 3 apricots, pitted • 1 orange • 1 tsp. ground almonds • ½ cup soy milk • sliced almonds, to serve

Juice the carrots, apricots and orange, then pour the juice into a blender and add the almonds and soy milk; process until smooth and creamy. Serve decorated with sliced almonds.

HEALTH BENEFITS
*Nutrient-dense almonds are rich in **protein and fiber** to help **stabilize blood sugar** and **aid elimination**. They are also a good source of **vitamin E** (a wonderful **skin nutrient**), as well as **energizing B-vitamins, magnesium, iron and zinc**.*

Nutritional analysis per serving: *Calories 173kcal • Protein 6.9g • Carbohydrates 26.1g [of which sugars 24g] • Fat 5.3g*

chlorophyll wonder

This medley of nutritious greens provides plenty of cleansing chlorophyll and protein to invigorate your body. It is low in calories and rich in electrolytes — ionized salt molecules which fire off the electrical impulses that enable your cells to communicate with one another. This is a powerfully revitalizing juice that can also eliminate toxins and reduce bloating.

1 celery stick • 1 handful of spinach leaves • 1 handful of kale leaves • 1 handful of sprouts, such as alfalfa • 2 apples • ½ cucumber

Juice all the vegetables and fruit together.

HEALTH BENEFITS
*Strongly alkaline celery is a **great detoxifying food** and is **calming for the digestion**. A well-known **diuretic**, celery's potassium–sodium electrolyte balance helps to **avoid water retention** and to **reduce blood pressure**. Celery is also **rich in B-vitamins and vitamin C**.*

Nutritional analysis per serving: *Calories 113kcal • Protein 5.7g • Carbohydrates 19.8g [of which sugars 18.4g] • Fat 1.6g*

gazpacho smoothie

Gazpacho is the name given to a tomato-based soup from Spain that is served refreshingly ice-cold. Here, the soup becomes a creamy-tasting juice that makes a complete meal in a glass. Because it's so satisfying, the juice helps to control any hunger pangs and provides a natural pick-me-up when your energy levels might be flagging.

1 red bell pepper, halved, seeded and cored • 1 carrot • ¼ red onion • 1 garlic clove • 2 tomatoes • ice cubes, to serve

Juice all the ingredients, then serve over ice.

HEALTH BENEFITS
*Onions are rich in **sulfur** to support **liver function** and help clear out toxins. They contain allicin and other **powerful natural antibiotics**, which help **fight off infections** (including parasites that can disturb digestive health). Red onions are particularly rich in **quercetin**, which has **anti-inflammatory and protective benefits**.*

Nutritional analysis per serving: *Calories 91kcal • Protein 2.9g • Carbohydrate 18.3g [of which sugars 17.1g] • Fat 1.2g*

parsley pleaser >

If you feel a bit bloated, have overindulged or need a quick spring clean, try this green magic. Parsley is an effective diuretic to help ease fluid retention, while apple is a great cleanser – and together they are superbly detoxifying. The baby spinach leaves will give you an energy lift.

1 large handful of flat-leaf parsley • 5½oz. baby spinach leaves • ½ cucumber • 2 apples • ice cubes, to serve

Juice all the ingredients, then serve over ice.

HEALTH BENEFITS
*Spinach is **packed with iron, vitamin C and folic acid** for **healthy blood cells**, making it a perfect **fatigue fighter**. It is also rich in **chlorophyll**, a substance that, together with the fiber in this juice, acts as an effective **cleanser and detoxifier**.*

Nutritional analysis per serving: *Calories 117kcal • Protein 5.9g • Carbohydrates 20.6g [of which sugars 19.3g] • Fat 1.5g*

mango no-tox

This nourishing and cleansing smoothie is both refreshing and sweet. The mango is packed with detoxifying properties that will boost your weight loss plan. Adding a small spoonful of flaxseed helps stabilize blood sugar and increases the fiber content to speed up detoxification.

1 apple • ½ cucumber • 2 celery sticks • ½ mango, peeled, pitted and chopped • ½ tsp. ground flaxseed

Juice the apple, cucumber and celery. Pour the juice into a blender, add the mango and flaxseed and process until smooth.

HEALTH BENEFITS
*Mango is rich in **soluble fiber**, which **lowers cholesterol**, and **insoluble fiber**, which **aids elimination**. Loaded with the **antioxidant vitamins A, C and E**, mango helps **protect against oxidative damage** and **support the liver** in its work neutralizing and **removing toxins** from your body.*

Nutritional analysis per serving: *Calories 109kcal • Protein 2.7g • Carbohydrates 22.2g [of which sugars 19.9g] • Fat 1.7g*

mulled fruit reviver

This warming juice is a hearty pick-me-up. Blending in the berries adds fiber to support digestive health and packs in plenty of health-promoting antioxidants. You could try this juice as a delicious, healthy alternative to mulled wine over the festive season, too.

7oz. seedless black grapes • 2 red plums • ½in. piece of gingerroot, peeled • ½ tsp. Manuka honey or agave nectar • ¼ cup mixed berries • ¼ tsp. cinnamon • 1 star anise • 2 cloves • ½ cinnamon stick, plus 1 stick to decorate

Juice the grapes, plums and ginger. Put the juice, honey, berries and ground cinnamon into a blender and process until smooth. Pour the blended juice into a pan, add the whole spices and warm through gently without boiling. Strain and serve warm, with a cinnamon stick for stirring.

HEALTH BENEFITS
*Grapes have a high water content, making them useful for **tackling constipation** and **detoxifying the gut**. Black and red grapes are also packed with **flavonoids**, which are **anti-inflammatory** and provide **protection against heart disease and cancer**.*

Nutritional analysis per serving: *Calories 165kcal • Protein 1.5g • Carbohydrates 41.8g [of which sugars 39.8g] • Fat 0.4g*

< cucumber cleanser

Cucumber has a high water content and is low in calories, making it a star ingredient for any slimming juice. In this juice grapefruit adds sweetness, as well as citric acid, which is an excellent digestive aid. A spoonful of sunflower seeds increases the protein content and levels of essential fats to support your metabolism.

1 white grapefruit, peeled • 1 cucumber • 2 celery sticks • 3 lettuce leaves, plus extra leaf to decorate • 2 tsp. sunflower seeds • ice cubes, to serve

Juice the fruit and vegetables. Put the juice and sunflower seeds into a blender and process until smooth. Serve over ice, decorated with a lettuce leaf.

HEALTH BENEFITS
*Cucumber contains **sulfur and silicon** – minerals that **support kidney and liver function** to aid elimination and tackle fluid retention. It is also rich in **potassium**, which helps maintain a **healthy fluid balance**.*

Nutritional analysis per serving: *Calories 136kcal • Protein 5.4g • Carbohydrates 17.1g [of which sugars 15g] • Fat 5.3g*

sweet fennel >

This juice has a distinctive, sweet anise flavor. An essential addition to your slimming portfolio, the ingredients in the juice provide flavonoids, which have been shown to ward off belly fat by improving the body's metabolic profile.

1 fennel bulb • 2 celery sticks • 2 apples • 1 handful of flat-leaf parsley • 1 tsp. psyllium husks

Juice the vegetables, fruit and herbs. Pour the juice into a blender, add the psyllium husks and process to combine.

HEALTH BENEFITS
*Fennel is a well-known **digestive aid**, because it is rich in **potassium and fiber** that boost elimination and **reduce fluid retention**. It also **improves fat digestion** by stimulating the gall bladder and increasing the flow of bile. The juice contains the **protective antioxidants** flavonoids, quercetin and rutin, plus **liver-supportive glucosinolates** (in the parsley).*

Nutritional analysis per serving: *Calories 93kcal • Protein 2.8g • Carbohydrates 20.1g [of which sugars 19.6g] • Fat 0.7g*

< cherry healer

This is a great juice for speeding up elimination. Cherries are high in potassium and low in sodium, so help control fluid levels in the body, while celery is an effective diuretic which helps flush out waste products and tackle fluid retention. Plain yogurt is a great source of protein and helps the body burn fat, while preserving muscle to help you develop a leaner, slimmer look.

4oz. cherries, pitted • 2 apples • 1 lemon • 2 celery sticks • 4 tbsp. low-fat plain yogurt

Juice the cherries, apples, lemon and celery. Pour the juice into a blender, add the yogurt and process until smooth.

HEALTH BENEFITS
*Plain yogurt contains **beneficial bacteria** that help **maintain the acid–alkali balance** of your body, **enhance immunity and aid digestion**. A good source of **tryptophan** (the precursor to the feel-good hormone serotonin), plain yogurt can **lift your mood** to help **keep you motivated** during the Juice Week.*

Nutritional analysis per serving: *Calories 110kcal • Protein 5g • Carbohydrates 21.4g [of which sugars 20.4g] • Fat 1g*

< ruby crush

Sweet, with a subtle, tart taste, this beautiful crimson juice bursts with protective antioxidants and vitamin C, plus bug-fighting chemicals, making it a soothing juice for your digestive tract. Serve it over ice for a cooling drink or turn it into a winter warmer by heating it gently with festive spices, such as cinnamon, star anise and cloves.

1²/₃ cups fresh or frozen cranberries, plus a few extra to decorate • 1 orange, peeled • 9oz. strawberries • 1 tsp. aloe vera juice • ice cubes, to serve

Juice all the fruit, then stir in the aloe vera juice. Serve over ice, decorated with two or three whole cranberries.

HEALTH BENEFITS
*Cranberries contain a **wealth of antioxidants** which promote health and **fight oxidative stress**. Rich in **proanthocyanidins**, they help keep the **urinary tract healthy**. They also help prevent harmful pathogens, such as Helicobacter pylori, from causing gastrointestinal problems.*

Nutritional analysis per serving: *Calories 138kcal • Protein 4g • Carbohydrates 31.1g [of which sugars 30.6g] • Fat 0.5g*

lean lychee

Superbly nutritious and refreshing, this juice contains low-calorie celery to tackle fluid retention and bloating, and lychees, which are traditionally used for their hydrating, diuretic and digestive qualities. Guava gives a vitamin-C boost and adds a wonderfully creamy texture.

1 guava • 2 celery sticks • 1 pear • 10 lychees, shelled and seeded • ice cubes, to serve

Juice the guava, celery and pear. Pour the juice into a blender, add the lychees and process until smooth. Serve over ice.

HEALTH BENEFITS
*Lychees provide plenty of **vitamin C and protective antioxidants**, especially flavonoids, which **boost immunity health** and help **strengthen the circulatory system**.*

Nutritional analysis per serving: *Calories 129kcal • Protein 2.4g • Carbohydrates 30.6g [of which sugars 30.3g] • Fat 0.6g*

lemon refresher

Try diluting this delicious juice with hot water to give you a boost in the morning, or with sparkling water for something more refreshing on a warm day. An effective digestive tonic, ginger adds a spicy kick. This is also a great juice to drink if you ever need to quell nausea and settle your stomach.

3 apples • 1 lemon, peeled • 1in. piece of gingerroot, peeled • sparkling water or hot water, to serve

Juice all the ingredients, then dilute with the water of your choice to serve.

HEALTH BENEFITS
*Apples contain soluble fiber known as **pectin**, which **binds to toxins** and helps eliminate them from the body. Fiber can also encourage the proliferation of **healthy bacteria** in the bowel, **stabilize blood-sugar levels** and **lower cholesterol**. Freshly pressed apple juice provides **malic acid**, which your cells use for **energy production**.*

Nutritional analysis per serving: *Calories 100kcal • Protein 1g • Carbohydrates 25g [of which sugars 24.4g] • Fat 0.2g*

minted greens >

Cleansing and calming for the digestive tract, this refreshing juice contains mint, a superb digestive aid that helps settle hyperacidity and improve bowel function, and lemon and apple, which are well-known cleansing fruits that stimulate waste elimination and fat breakdown. Kiwi is rich in natural sugars, making this juice a fantastic pick-me-up.

2 kiwifruits, peeled • 1 apple • ½ cucumber • ½ lemon, peeled • 1 handful of spinach leaves • 3 mint leaves, plus extra sprig to decorate • ice cubes, to serve

Juice all the ingredients together and serve over ice, decorated with a sprig of mint.

HEALTH BENEFITS
*Kiwifruits are high in fiber for **blood-sugar control** and rich in the enzyme actinidin, which **helps your body digest protein**. Packed full with the **antioxidant vitamins A, C, E** and **beta-carotene**, kiwi **nourishes your immune system** and helps your body **deal with stress**.*

Nutritional analysis per serving: *Calories 125kcal • Protein 4.6g • Carbohydrates 24.6g [of which sugars 22.6g] • Fat 1.3g*

< stress tonic

This juice is a superbly calming tonic, making it the perfect choice if you're feeling anxious or stressed – try sipping it during the evening to help you relax and unwind before bedtime. The soy yogurt in the tonic provides protein to help stabilize your blood-sugar levels.

4½oz. strawberries • 1 pear • 1 apple • ½ tsp. tahini • 1 tsp. wheat germ • 2 tbsp. soy yogurt • ⅓ cup soy milk • ice cubes, to serve

Juice the fruit, then pour into a blender, add the remaining ingredients and process until smooth. Serve over ice.

HEALTH BENEFITS
*Soy yogurt provides **beneficial bacteria** to help maintain the **correct acidity in your bowel**, as well as **dietary fiber to aid your digestion**. It is also rich in **B-vitamins**, which are essential nutrients for the **proper functioning of your adrenal glands** (responsible for producing the stress hormone adrenaline) and **isoflavones**, compounds that can **protect against certain cancers**.*

Nutritional analysis per serving: *Calories 225kcal • Protein 8g • Carbohydrates 38.5g [of which sugars 35.2g] • Fat 5.3g*

raspberry twist

Fruity, cleansing and energizing, this juice is perfect if you need a pick-me-up.
All the fruits are rich in soluble fiber, including pectin, which helps curb your
appetite while stimulating elimination. The hemp seeds create a creamy
texture and are packed full with essential fats that boost your metabolism.

1 apple • 1 pink grapefruit, peeled • 2 cups raspberries • 1 tbsp. shelled hemp seeds

Juice the apple and grapefruit. Pour the juice into a blender, add the raspberries
and hemp seeds and process until creamy.

HEALTH BENEFITS
*All berries burst with vitamins and antioxidants, but raspberries are also rich in **ellagic acid**,
which is known for its **anti-cancer properties**. Pink grapefruit, like other grapefruits, is rich in
antioxidants and helps **boost liver function and blood circulation**. Hemp seeds are particularly
rich in **calcium and magnesium**, which are essential minerals for **bone health**.*

*Nutritional analysis per serving: Calories 114kcal • Protein 5g • Carbohydrates 16g [of which
sugars 15.1g] • Fat 3.9g*

chili tomato

Low in carbohydrates, which your body converts to sugar, this juice is perfect for stabilizing your energy levels and preventing the highs and lows of blood-sugar fluctuation. The juice's high water and potassium content make it ideal for cleansing your system and so also aid the slimming process.

4 tomatoes • 2 celery sticks • ½ cucumber • a pinch of cayenne pepper • a splash Tabasco sauce

Juice the vegetables, then season the juice with cayenne pepper and Tabasco to taste.

HEALTH BENEFITS
*Cayenne pepper and the capsaicin in the Tabasco are both **circulatory stimulants**, boosting the body's metabolic rate and **speeding up cleansing and elimination**. The juice is rich in protective **beta-carotene, vitamin C and zinc** to help **strengthen your immune system**.*

Nutritional analysis per serving: *Calories 70kcal • Protein 3.4g • Carbohydrates 11.5g [of which sugar 10.7g] • Fat 1.4g*

juice for life

If you've succeeded at the Weekend Juice Blitz or the Juice Week and now you want some slimming juice recipes for the longer term, the delicious, health-promoting juices and smoothies of the Juice for Life program are for you. Every juice is designed to be easy to put together so that you can work it into even the busiest schedule. The juices provide essential vitamins, minerals, enzymes and phytochemicals that maximize your health and keep your metabolism ticking over at optimum levels to prevent weight gain and even achieve gentle, long-term weight loss. If staying slim, optimizing your well-being, feeling great and eating healthily are what you're aiming for, just one of these juices every day will help you realize your goals. Fire up your body for the day ahead with a Green Tea Cocktail, or stay away from the cookie jar by drinking the creamy, sustaining Mandarin and Mango Lassi. These and all the juices in this chapter have only one goal – to keep you lean, slim and beautiful.

< melon cooler, page 91

the juice for life program

I want to make staying slim as easy for you as possible, and that's why the Juice for Life program doesn't try to be rigid or difficult to achieve, but instead aims to be something you can make a simple part of your life.

To help make long-term optimal health easy to achieve, when you're following the Juice for Life program, try to stick to the principles set out in the Weekend Juice Blitz and Juice Week chapters (see pages 22 and 46–47) at least 80 percent of the time. This means you can be less strict on yourself 20 percent of the time to allow for the odd indulgence. When you're juicing for life, you can eat red meat or dairy foods, and drink alcohol or caffeinated drinks – just not every day.

Choosing your juices The Juice for Life program means including a freshly made juice or smoothie every day. Try to make sure that over the course of each week you drink juices in a rainbow of colors. You might prefer the red or orange juices, but make sure you get in a few green juices too, since these support your liver's cleansing work (which helps fight cellulite and fat). If you have specific health goals,

feel free to include juices from the Beauty, Power and Immunity chapters.

If at any time you feel your motivation is waning, use the Weekend Juice Blitz or Juice Week to get you back on track.

Getting started To get you started on your own Juice for Life program, I've devised two sample days for you to follow. They show how you only need to make simple changes to your diet and work in just one juice a day to stay on the road to a slim and fabulous you. Don't forget to incorporate a cleansing treatment (see page 14) every other week (or more often if you can manage it) to give your efforts a boost, and incorporate a regular workout routine, too. Twice a week, do 30 minutes of resistance or weight training; and three or four times a week, do 30 minutes' cardiovascular exercise that makes you slightly breathless.

juice for life plan sample days

day one

On waking A cup of hot water with juice of ½ lemon

Breakfast Creamy Cacao Nut Shake **(page 85)**

Mid-morning snack 1 peach; 1 handful of almonds

Lunch Grilled chicken salad: Grill 1 chicken breast. Serve with 1 large handful of mixed greens with 2 chopped marinated artichoke hearts, 1 handful of black olives, 2 cherry tomatoes, and ½ red pepper chopped. Dress with lemon juice and a dash of sesame oil and soy sauce

Mid-afternoon snack Carrot and celery sticks with 4½oz. cottage cheese and 2 oat cakes

Dinner Shrimp curry: Chop ½ red onion, then sauté with 1 tsp. curry paste and 1 chopped garlic clove. Cube ½ sweet potato, dice 1 carrot and add to the pan with 1 cup coconut milk; simmer for 10 minutes. Add 1 handful of green beans, 3½oz. cooked shrimp and 7oz. canned chopped tomatoes. Bring to a boil, reduce the heat to low and simmer for 5 minutes. Serve with ½ cup cooked brown basmati rice. A bowl of berries and 3 tbsp. low-fat plain yogurt

day two

On waking Green tea

Breakfast Simmer 2 tbsp. rolled oats in ¼ cup water until soft. Add a pinch of cinnamon, 1 handful of blueberries and 2 tbsp. mixed seeds. Top with 2 tbsp. low-fat plain yogurt

Mid-morning snack Goji Burst **(page 86)**

Lunch Curried lentil soup (see page 48) with salad of ½ sliced fennel bulb, 1 grated apple, 1 handful of walnuts and 1 handful of watercress, arugula or mâche. To dress: 1 tbsp. orange juice and 1 tsp. olive oil

Mid-afternoon snack 2 rye crackers spread with almond butter

Dinner Roast salmon: Dice ½ butternut squash. Roast with halved ½ red onion and ½ red bell pepper for 15 minutes. Stir in 1 handful of asparagus; top with 1 salmon fillet. Drizzle with olive oil and lemon. Bake for 10 minutes until the salmon is cooked through.

< creamy cacao nut shake

This indulgent-tasting smoothie bursts with nutrients to keep you energized throughout the day and makes a perfect replacement for breakfast. The nuts give the shake a high protein content, which balances your blood-sugar levels, keeping your mind alert and in focus.

scant 1 cup almond milk • 1 tbsp. raw cacao nibs or powder • ½ small banana • ½ tsp. vanilla extract • 1 tsp. agave nectar • a pinch of cinnamon, to serve

Process all the ingredients in a blender until smooth and creamy. Serve sprinkled with the cinnamon.

HEALTH BENEFITS
*Raw cacao is unprocessed and unheated, and so contains far more **antioxidants** than processed cocoa, and more than even most fruits and vegetables. It is particularly rich in **magnesium** (which you need for **muscle function and relaxation**) and **arginine**, an amino acid that helps **maintain muscle mass**. It is also packed with the **amino acids tryptophan and phenylethylamine**, which can **boost mood**.*

Nutritional analysis per serving: *Calories 181kcal • Protein 3.8g • Carbohydrates 28g [of which sugars 11.6g] • Fat 9.2g*

goji burst

This juice is the perfect combination of quick energy fix and long-lasting power drink. A creamy, dairy-free smoothie, it is packed with antioxidants, B-vitamins and plenty of protein to combat fatigue. Serve it as a quick breakfast shake or a mid-morning snack.

½oz. dried goji berries • 1 orange, peeled • ½ persimmon • ½ tbsp. almonds • ⅓ cup raspberries • ½ small banana

Soak the goji berries in scant ¾ cup water for 15 minutes. Juice the orange. Put the juice and the remaining ingredients, including goji berries and their soaking liquid, into a blender and process until smooth.

HEALTH BENEFITS
*Goji berries contain **all the essential amino acids** (those we have to derive from food), as well as numerous trace minerals, including **zinc, iron, calcium and selenium** for **immune health and energy production**. Ounce for ounce, they have **more beta-carotene than carrots**.*

Nutritional analysis per serving: *Calories 210kcal • Protein 6.3g • Carbohydrates 41.6g [of which sugars 25.2g] • Fat 4.6g*

green tea cocktail

Powerfully cleansing and protective, this juice will fire up your body for the day and speed up the elimination of toxins. Drinking green tea has been shown to stimulate metabolism and your body's ability to burn fat – this means that less fat is stored around your midriff. It is delicious drunk warm or cold.

3 apples • 1 lemon, peeled • ½in. piece of gingerroot, peeled • scant ⅔ cup brewed green tea, warm or cooled

Juice the apples, lemon and ginger. Stir the juice into the green tea.

HEALTH BENEFITS
*Green tea contains **health-boosting antioxidants**, including flavonoids and catechins, which can help **support heart health** and may **protect against cancer**. Its tannin content is **good for digestive complaints**, while the theanine in green tea can help **alleviate stress and improve mental alertness**. The ginger in this juice **aids circulation** and digestive health.*

Nutritional analysis per serving: *Calories 101kcal • Protein 1.3g • Carbohydrates 24.7g [of which sugars 23.5g] • Fat 0.3g*

blueberry and açaí berry shake >

For effective weight loss this shake has it all. Bursting with powerful antioxidants, including anthocyanidins, it supports liver enzyme systems to aid the removal of toxins and waste from your body. Rich in soluble fiber, such as pectin, and probiotic yogurt, it helps satisfy hunger and stabilize your blood-sugar levels, therefore boosting energy and curbing cravings. Pectin can also help absorb toxins from the digestive tract, making this shake a valuable cleanser. Because it is low in calories but satisfying, this drink is an excellent meal replacement if you want to lose weight.

²/₃ cup blueberries, plus 4 or 5 extra to decorate • ½ cup raspberries • ¼ cup açaí or pomegranate juice • 4 tbsp. low-fat plain yogurt • ice cubes, to serve

Process all the ingredients in a blender until smooth. Serve in a long glass over ice, decorated with four or five whole blueberries.

HEALTH BENEFITS
*Blueberries contain **pterostilbene and pectin**, which are thought to help **reduce blood-cholesterol** levels, **cleanse the body** and **assist toxin removal**, while strengthening your capillaries – **great for tackling cellulite and stubborn fat**.*

Nutritional analysis per serving: *Calories 93kcal • Protein 3.8g • Carbohydrates 17.9g [of which sugars 17.9g] • Fat 0.8g*

< peaches and cream

A beautiful blend of vanilla and spices, this smoothie is a dreamy sensation. Protein-rich almonds and the bananas provide a low-fat, low-calorie creaminess and it makes a nourishing, quick breakfast drink or mid-morning snack.

1 peach, plus extra to decorate • ½ banana • ½ tsp. vanilla extract • 1 tbsp. almond butter • ½ tsp. agave nectar • a pinch of cinnamon • a pinch of pumpkin pie spice • ice cubes, to serve

Put all the ingredients into a blender, add ½ cup water, and process until smooth. Serve over ice, decorated with a slice of peach.

HEALTH BENEFITS
*Peaches are rich in **flavonoids, lycopene, beta-carotene and vitamin C** for immunity support and **cell regeneration**. They also provide **folic acid and B-vitamins**, which **help revitalize your body**.*

Nutritional analysis per serving: *Calories 169kcal • Protein 4.8g • Carbohydrates 20.8g [of which sugars 17.8g] • Fat 8g*

melon cooler

Sweet and refreshing with a sour edge, this is the perfect juice to wake up your taste buds in the morning. It is a light, low-calorie juice that will help keep your diet on track. Try it diluted with sparkling water as a revitalizing summer drink.

7oz. cantaloupe melon, peeled • 1 lime, peeled • 2 mint leaves • 1 pear, plus extra pear quarter to decorate • ice cubes, to serve

Juice all the ingredients, then serve over ice and decorate with a pear quarter.

HEALTH BENEFITS
*The orange-fleshed cantaloupe melon is an excellent source of **beta-carotene and vitamin C** – powerful nutrients that help **maintain healthy skin and protect your body from free-radical damage**. A rich source of **potassium**, cantaloupe melons help **regulate blood pressure** and maintain a **healthy fluid balance**, too.*

Nutritional analysis per serving: *Calories 112kcal • Protein 1.9g • Carbohydrates 26.6g [of which sugars 25.2g] • Fat 0.4g*

carotene booster

If you need a burst of energy during the day, sip this sensational creamy juice, which is rich in rejuvenating vitamin C and carotenes. The peanut butter offers a good dose of protein and fats to help provide a steady release of fuel for your body's cells and keep you feeling more satisfied, so that you avoid unhealthy snacking.

½ small sweet potato • 7oz. cantaloupe melon, peeled • 2 carrots • 1 tsp. salt- and sugar-free smooth peanut butter

Juice the sweet potato, melon and carrots. Pour the juice into a blender, add the peanut butter and process until creamy.

HEALTH BENEFITS
*Peanut butter packs a really nutritional punch – it is rich in antioxidants, including **resveratrol and vitamin E**, and other **heart-protective nutrients**, such as folate and monounsaturated fats. Cantaloupe melon and carrots are some of the **top sources of beta-carotene**, which your body converts to vitamin A and is essential for a **healthy immune system**.*

Nutritional analysis per serving: *Calories 239kcal • Protein 5.1g • Carbohydrates 47.6 [of which sugars 22.2g] • Fat 4.5g*

super greens >

Light and refreshing, the burst of chlorophyll and protein in this juice is incredibly nourishing and helps cleanse your body and boost liver function. It's a wonderful juice to keep you feeling light and vibrant.

1 large handful of kale leaves • 1 large handful of spinach leaves • 2 pears • 1 lemon, peeled • scant ⅔ cup coconut water • ice cubes, to serve

Juice the vegetables and fruit, then stir in the coconut water and serve over ice.

HEALTH BENEFITS
*Coconut water is often called the "Fluid of Life", as it contains a **balanced proportion of the electrolytes** potassium, calcium, magnesium and sodium, which help the body achieve **correct fluid balance**. Wonderfully revitalizing, it is the **perfect isotonic drink** for rehydration following exercise.*

Nutritional analysis per serving: *Calories 176kcal • Protein 3.7g • Carbohydrates 38.7g [of which sugars 30.5g] • Fat 1.4g*

bug blaster

If you're feeling a little run down, whiz up this delicious smoothie to keep the bugs at bay, while at the same time preventing cravings and supporting your digestive health. The smoothie is rich in vitamin C and protective antioxidants, as well as healthy bacteria (from the yogurt) to support immune health. Deliciously thick, it provides a superfast pick-me-up meal when time is short.

½ tsp. wheat germ • ½ tbsp. rolled oats • 3 pecan halves • 4oz. strawberries • ½ banana • ½ cup orange juice • 4 tbsp. low-fat plain yogurt

Put the wheat germ, oats and nuts in a large non-stick frying pan. Cook over medium heat, stirring occasionally until lightly toasted; let cool. Put the rest of the ingredients and half the toasted oat mixture into a blender and process until smooth and creamy. Pour into a glass and top with the rest of the oat mixture.

HEALTH BENEFITS
*Wheat germ is a highly concentrated source of nutrients including **protein, B-vitamins, vitamin E** and the minerals **zinc, selenium and magnesium**. It is also a great source of **fiber**. Oats and nuts provide plenty of zinc, too, which is an essential nutrient for a **healthy immune system**.*

Nutritional analysis per serving: *Calories 247kcal • Protein 7.5g • Carbohydrates 32.6g [of which sugars 24.3g] • Fat 10.4g*

avocado whip

Avocado might seem like a strange ingredient to add to a juice, but it creates a creamy texture and blends well with stronger-tasting fruits. This drink will keep your energy at a good level through the day and, because avocado helps slow down the flow of glucose into your cells, it is a great drink for keeping hunger pangs at bay.

5½oz. pineapple • ½ lime, peeled • ½ avocado, peeled and pitted • ½ mango, peeled and pitted • 2 tsp. shelled hemp seeds • ice cubes, to serve

Juice the pineapple and lime. Pour the juice into a blender, add the remaining ingredients and scant ½ cup water, and process until smooth. Add a little more water if the mixture is too thick. Serve over ice.

HEALTH BENEFITS
*Avocados are among the most nutritious fruits available. They are rich in **healthy fats** and packed with the **antioxidant vitamins A, C and E to protect cells**, and **energizing B-vitamins to support adrenal function** during times of stress.*

Nutritional analysis per serving: *Calories 258kcal • Protein 5.3g • Carbohydrates 28.1g [of which sugars 24.8g] • Fat 14.9g*

< pomegranate power

Pomegranates are packed with antioxidants, which together with the maca root in this juice, provide an energizing drink to heal and protect your body. Refreshing and revitalizing, this is a perfect juice to boost your energy levels and keep you feeling simply amazing all day.

1 pomegranate, seeds and pulp • 1 apple • 2½oz. cherries, pitted • scant ⅔ cup coconut water • 1 tsp. maca root powder

Juice the pomegranate and apple. Pour the juice into a blender, add the remaining ingredients and process until smooth.

HEALTH BENEFITS
*Maca is a root from Peru and is sometimes referred to as Peruvian ginseng. Known as **an adaptogen**, it helps the body **rebalance in times of stress** and is an amazing source of vitamins, minerals (especially calcium), enzymes and protein. It can also help **regulate female hormones**, making it useful in **tackling menopausal and premenstrual symptoms**.*

Nutritional analysis per serving: *Calories 167kcal • Protein 2.8g • Carbohydrates 39.6g [of which sugars 28.4g] • Fat 0.4g*

vegetable cocktail

If you're on the go, this sweet, light vegetable juice is perfect as a refreshing snack or as part of a low-calorie lunch. It is packed with slow-releasing energy to keep those hunger pangs away.

3 tomatoes • 2 carrots • 2 oranges • ¼ cucumber • 1 handful of basil leaves

Juice all the ingredients together.

HEALTH BENEFITS
*This juice brims with **phytonutrients** to **prevent chronic diseases**, such as cancer. Fragrant basil is well known for its **anti-microbial** effects – its essential oils help **reduce inflammation and kill harmful bacteria**; basil can also reduce the risk of food poisoning and may **calm digestive upsets**.*

Nutritional analysis per serving: *Calories 158kcal • Protein 5.1g • Carbohydrates 33.9g [of which sugars 31.6g] • Fat 1.2g*

cranberry protector

The coconut milk in this creamy, pink juice is a rich source of medium-chain triglycerides, which are known to increase calorie burning. This means that they promote energy production rather than being stored as fat. Adding a spoonful of almonds to the juice provides protein to sustain you and essential fats to aid your metabolism.

1 pear • 1¼ cups fresh or frozen cranberries • scant ⅔ cup coconut milk • 1 tsp. ground almonds • 1 tsp. Manuka honey

Juice the pear and cranberries together. Pour the juice into a blender, add the remaining ingredients and process until smooth and creamy.

HEALTH BENEFITS
*Coconut milk is easily digested and absorbed and a great **boost for digestive and immune health**. It is rich in lauric acid, which has **anti-viral and anti-microbial properties**, and caprylic acid, which is **anti-fungal**, making it an **all-round protective** food. Cranberries are rich in **immunity-boosting antioxidants** and are particularly soothing if you have a urinary tract infection. The Manuka honey in this drink contains anti-microbial properties and will give an **instant burst of energy** when your reserves are low.*

Nutritional analysis per serving: *Calories 164kcal • Protein 2.4g • Carbohydrates 32.7g [of which sugars 31g] • Fat 3.5g*

peach clean

Summery and fruity, this peach smoothie is a great source of natural sugars and soluble fiber to stabilize your blood sugar and keep your energy levels high. Adding a handful of seeds or nuts provides protein and essential fats to support your liver function and boost your metabolism to aid weight loss.

2 peaches, pitted • 1 carrot • 1 orange, peeled • 1 small banana • 2 tsp. sunflower seeds

Juice the peaches, carrot and orange. Pour the juice into a blender, add the banana and seeds and process until smooth. Add a little water to dilute, if necessary.

HEALTH BENEFITS
*Packed with **vitamin C and beta-carotene**, peaches can help **support immune health** and nourish your skin for **a more radiant, glowing you**. They are also rich in **potassium** to **support fluid balance** and help **regulate your blood pressure**.*

Nutritional analysis per serving: *Calories 242kcal • Protein 6g • Carbohydrates 45.2g [of which sugars 40.4g] • Fat 5.4g*

carrot, lemon & spice

This nourishing, antioxidant-rich juice is full of natural sugars to pep up your energy levels and help you sail through times when you might be faced with the temptation of unhealthy, sweet snacks. The ginger in the juice is thought to boost your metabolism – which is great news for slimmers who want to speed up calorie burning.

1 lemon, peeled • 1 pear • 3 carrots • 3 celery sticks • ½in. piece of gingerroot, peeled • ice cubes, to serve

Jucie all the ingredients, mix well and serve over ice.

HEALTH BENEFITS
*A well-known digestive aid, gingerroot can help **relieve indigestion and nausea**. Its **powerful gingerols** possess anti-inflammatory properties known to help **reduce pain and inflammation** and **alleviate asthma**.*

Nutritional analysis per serving: *Calories 57kcal • Protein 1.7g • Carbohydrates 11.6g [of which sugars 10.4g] • Fat 0.7g*

tropical twist >

This juice is guaranteed to lift your mood and perk you up if you're starting to flag. Blending the mango (rather than juicing it) provides the drink with plenty of soluble fiber to encourage your body to eliminate toxins and to support your gut health.

2 kiwifruits, peeled • 3½oz. pineapple, peeled • ½ mango, peeled, pitted and chopped • 1 tbsp. lime juice

Juice the kiwifruit and pineapple. Pour the juice into a blender, add the mango and lime juice and process until smooth. Dilute the juice with water to taste.

HEALTH BENEFITS
*Limes are packed with **vitamin C** and **bioflavonoids** that support liver function and **speed up detoxification**. They also help **strengthen blood vessels**, giving a great boost for **glowing, healthy skin**, and are a good source of **cancer-fighting limonene** and **cholesterol-lowering pectin**. The enzyme **bromelain** in the pineapple will **aid your digestion**.*

Nutritional analysis per serving: *Calories 144kcal • Protein 2.3g • Carbohydrates 33.6g [of which sugars 31.5g] • Fat 1g*

< perfect pepper

Sweet and creamy, this juice has a spoonful of tahini (sesame paste) to provide protein and essential fats. These will help sustain you throughout the day and support your metabolism.

1 red bell pepper, halved, seeded and cored, plus extra to decorate • 2 carrots • ½ sweet potato • 1 tsp. tahini

Juice the pepper, carrots and sweet potato. Pour the juice into a blender, add the tahini and process until smooth. Serve decorated with a slice of red pepper.

HEALTH BENEFITS
*Red bell peppers are loaded with **cancer-fighting lycopene** and immunity-boosting **beta-carotene** and **vitamin C**. These help **fight off infections, protect the lungs and promote skin health**. The tahini in the juice provides plenty of **calcium and magnesium for bone health**.*

Nutritional analysis per serving: *Calories 221kcal • Protein 4.2g • Carbohydrates 43.4g [of which sugars 18.5g] • Fat 4.5g*

toffee apple banana

Simple but packed with power, this smoothie has a wonderful toffee-like flavor from the mesquite powder. This is known to help stabilize blood sugar, by improving insulin function and slowing the rate of release of glucose into the body's cells, which in turn will help prevent hunger pangs. Using dates for sweetness provides soluble fiber and also slows down the release of sugars in the body.

1½ apples • 1½ small bananas • 3 dates • 1 tsp. almond butter • 1 tbsp. mesquite powder

Juice the apples. Pour the juice into a blender, add the remaining ingredients and ½ cup water; process until smooth.

HEALTH BENEFITS
*Mesquite powder is a traditional **North American superfood** made by grinding the seed pods of the mesquite tree. It is a **high-protein** food that is **rich in key minerals**, such as **calcium, magnesium, iron and zinc**.*

Nutritional analysis per serving: *Calories 257kcal • Protein 5.1g • Carbohydrates 48.5g [of which sugars 38.5g] • Fat 3.6g*

papaya blast >

Feeling a little sluggish? Try this enzyme booster. The pineapple and papaya in this juice provide bromelain and papain – enzymes that help boost digestion and stimulate the absorption and assimilation of nutrients in your gut.

5½oz. pineapple, peeled • 2 celery sticks • 2 mint leaves, plus extra sprig to decorate • ½ papaya, seeded and peeled

Juice the pineapple, celery and mint leaves. Pour the juice into a blender, add the papaya and process until smooth. Dilute with water to taste and decorate with a mint sprig.

HEALTH BENEFITS

*Soothing and calming, mint is a great digestive aid. It is **effective against many common digestive complaints,** including indigestion, wind and irregular bowel movements. It is also a popular **remedy for irritable bowel syndrome** and **alleviating abdominal cramps and pain**.*

Nutritional analysis per serving: Calories 94kcal • Protein 1.9g • Carbohydrates 21.3g [of which sugars 14.9g] • Fat 0.5g

< yellow roots

Cleansing and refreshing, this delicate juice balances fluid levels and alleviates fluid retention. The splash of ginger helps calm digestive upsets and ease any nausea from over-indulgences, while a spoonful of probiotic or glutamine powder helps support gut health.

1 pear • 2 parsnips • 4oz. celeriac, peeled • 7oz. cantaloupe melon, peeled • ½in. piece of gingerroot, peeled • 1 tsp. probiotic or glutamine powder

Juice all the food ingredients, then stir in the probiotic powder.

HEALTH BENEFITS
*Parsnips provide plenty of natural sugars to **raise energy levels** and are rich in the **antioxidant vitamins C and E**, plus a wealth of phytochemicals, which **tackle the free radicals associated with aging**. They also contain plenty of **potassium** which helps **regulate fluid levels**.*

Nutritional analysis per serving: Calories 181kcal • Protein 4.5g • Carbohydrates 38.8g [of which sugars 31.1g] • Fat 1.7g

celery spice

Try this stimulating juice on days when you want to eat lightly. The combination of pears, celery and fennel is beneficial for digestive health and altogether this is a great juice to help reduce fluid retention and bloating.

3 celery sticks • ½ fennel bulb • ½ cucumber • 2 sage leaves • an oregano sprig • 2 pears • Worcestershire sauce or tamari soy sauce

Juice all the ingredients. Serve with a dash of sauce, to taste.

HEALTH BENEFITS
*Oregano is a top **antioxidant-rich** herb, ounce for ounce offering **four times more protection than blueberries**. Known for its potent anti-microbial effects, oregano can **kill harmful bacteria, viruses and fungi** (including Candida albicans) and appears to be **beneficial for respiratory health**, too.*

Nutritional analysis per serving: Calories 151kcal • Protein 2.9g • Carbohydrates 34.5g [of which sugars 32g] • Fat 0.9g

citrus green cleanse

A citrus fruit grown in Jamaica, ugly fruit is a good source of soluble fiber and minerals and is wonderfully cleansing to help keep your skin smooth and glowing. Packed with protective antioxidants, this juice is the perfect antidote to stressful, dreary days when you need a quick lift.

2 oranges, peeled • 1 ugly fruit or white grapefruit, peeled • 1 zucchini • 3 broccoli florets • ½in. piece of gingerroot, peeled

Juice all the ingredients, then stir to combine.

HEALTH BENEFITS
*Citrus fruits are known for their immunity-boosting properties, because they are **packed full of bioflavonoids and vitamin C**, which help **stimulate the activity of your body's white blood cells**. The ginger in this juice helps **stimulate digestive function** and **circulation**.*

Nutritional analysis per serving: Calories 166kcal • Protein 7.2g • Carbohydrates 33.7g [of which sugars 31.7g] • Fat 1.1g

mandarin and mango lassi >

Using canned fruit in this tropical-tasting, refreshing shake makes it speedy to put together. Cashews add a good dose of protein to keep you fuller for longer. Try it at the end of a hard day or as a post-workout snack.

⅓ cup coconut milk • ¼ mango, peeled, pitted and chopped • 4½oz. canned mandarins • 1½ tbsp. cashews • ½ tsp. cardamom seeds • ice cubes, to serve

Drain the mandarins and reserve ⅓ cup of the juice. Process all the ingredients and the reserved juice in a blender until creamy. Serve over ice.

HEALTH BENEFITS
*Cashews are great **fatigue fighters**, being **rich in copper and iron** which help build your red blood cells. A good source of **magnesium and calcium**, they can help **strengthen bones and relax muscles**, while the **protein** in them is great for **muscle recovery and repair**.*

Nutritional analysis per serving: Calories 191kcal • Protein 4.5g • Carbohydrates 27.9g [of which sugars 24.5g] • Fat 7.7g

beauty juices

Whether you're looking to tackle cellulite, clear your complexion or keep those wrinkles at bay, adding fresh juice to your diet is a sure way to see results. Your skin is a fundamental part of your body's waste-management system. Drinking just one juice a day can help speed up the skin's cleansing processes to improve its clarity and texture and promote collagen formation to keep your skin supple. A daily juice can also add luster to your hair. The mouthwatering selection of nutrient-rich juices in this chapter is packed with beauty-boosting nutrients for healthy-looking, radiant skin, shiny hair – and strong nails, too. Start one day with a fruity Apricot Peach Whip to tackle those pimples and give yourself a beautiful glow. At lunch on another day you might try the delicious, sweet-tasting Purple Booster, with ingredients that protect your skin from the aging effects of free radicals. These and all the other juices in this chapter are here to make your beauty-care routine as delicious as it is effective.

< grape and lemon cleanse, page 125

the beauty juice program

Most of the women I know – myself included – spend a lot of time and money on beauty-care products that work from the outside in. We buy cosmetics, lotions and creams that make promises to reduce the signs of aging, tackle blemishes and add a shine to our hair.

However, what you eat can have a far more profound effect on your appearance. If you feed your body with the right nutrients, your skin and hair will glow with good health. And what is one of the easiest ways to boost your beauty nutrients? To make beauty juices part of your daily beauty routine.

Your skin is the largest organ in your body and a major route for the body's elimination of toxins. This means that it is also often the first place you see the consequences of a poor diet – pimples, dry skin and other blemishes can all be an indication that your body isn't getting the right kind of nutrients for good health. A diet that is rich in fruits and vegetables supports your liver in its bid to rid your body of toxins, which will help keep your skin clear. The vitamin C in fruits and vegetables is essential for the formation of collagen and elastin, which help keep your skin supple, flexible and looking young. As your diet improves, your skin cells multiply in the deep layers of your epidermis (the upper portion of your skin). Over roughly four weeks, these fresh, plump cells are pushed to the surface to keep you looking young.

Skin nutrients Many of the juices in this chapter include essential fatty acids, such as those found in nuts, seeds, seed oils and avocado. Your body's cells absorb these healthy fats to help keep your skin and hair moisturized. Along with many antioxidants, healthy fats are anti-inflammatory, too, which is important if you suffer from skin conditions such as rashes, eczema, or psoriasis. If you have dry skin or dandruff, the biotin (a B-vitamin) found in nuts, avocado and certain fruits and vegetables such as tomatoes and carrots, helps keep these problems at bay. Nuts and plain yogurt also contain zinc, which can help heal scars and broken skin. If acne or pimples are a concern for you, your skin may be producing too much sebum, the skin's natural moisturizer. Vitamin A (found in various vegetables and fruits, including carrots, greens and cantaloupe melon) can be useful in reducing sebum levels.

For long-term healthy aging and radiant looks, your diet needs sufficient protein to help repair and replenish skin and nail cells and to promote strong, glossy hair. This is why many of the juices in this chapter include protein in the form of yogurt, nuts and seeds.

Using the beauty juices To maximize the benefits of the beauty juices, I recommend you drink two or three of them daily for at least four weeks. You can combine them with any of the juice diet programs, or simply focus on including beauty juices alongside your usual, healthy diet if you prefer. Select juices to address your particular beauty concerns, or include a wide selection to gain all-round benefits. Below, I've outlined a sample day to guide you.

beauty juice sample day

Breakfast Apricot Peach Whip **(page 114)**

Mid-morning snack Vegetable sticks with guacamole dip

Lunch 2-egg omelet made with chopped mixed bell peppers, 1 handful of spinach and 2 chopped tomatoes; mixed salad. Bowl of blueberries topped with 2 tbsp. low-fat plain yogurt

Mid-afternoon snack Instant Botox **(page 122)**; 1 handful of pumpkin seeds

Dinner Wound Healer **(page 116)**. Grilled salmon with steamed broccoli, carrots and asparagus, and a baked sweet potato

apricot peach whip

purple booster >

The combination of fruit and soy in this juice provides plenty of energizing beta-carotene and protein to protect and heal your skin. If you're concerned about cellulite, the lecithin granules and omega oil help break down fat and stimulate metabolism.

This wonderfully thick, deep-red juice provides protection from oxidative damage associated with aging; its blended berries provide plenty of soluble fiber to encourage waste elimination for a cleaner, more radiant complexion.

5½oz. pineapple, peeled • 2 apricots, pitted • 1 small peach, pitted • 4oz. silken tofu • 1 tsp. lecithin granules • 1 tsp. omega 3-6-9 oil blend, or flaxseed oil

1 raw beet • 1 apple • 1⅓ cups mixed berries, such as blueberries and raspberries, plus 2 or 3 extra to decorate

Juice the pineapple. Put the juice and all the other ingredients into a blender and process until smooth and creamy.

Juice the beet and apple, then pour the juice into a blender and add the berries. Add scant ½ cup water and process until smooth. Decorate with the fresh berries.

HEALTH BENEFITS
*Lecithin granules, made from soy, can **speed up the breakdown of fats**, making them a useful ingredient for promoting **weight loss** and **lowering cholesterol**. They can also **support liver and gallbladder health**. Lecithin contains contains phosphatidylcholine, an essential component of cell membranes. Taken as a supplement, it is converted into choline, a vital nutrient for **improved brain function**.*

HEALTH BENEFITS
*Berries are an amazing source of **anthocyanidins**, antioxidants that **increase the potency of vitamin C**, which is important for your body's production of collagen to **keep your skin supple**.*

Nutritional analysis per serving: *Calories 102kcal • Protein 2.2g • Carbohydrates 23.8g [of which sugars 22.6g] • Fat 0.5g*

Nutritional analysis per serving: *Calories 220kcal • Protein 11.3g • Carbohydrates 27g [of which sugars 25.3g] • Fat 8.3g*

< wound healer

Including the mango in this juice boosts its fiber content to ensure your body eliminates waste products effectively, helping to leave your skin clear and fresh. Zinc and vitamin A are crucially important for healing skin wounds and this juice provides plenty of both.

5½oz. pineapple, peeled • 2½oz. strawberries • ½ mango, peeled, pitted and chopped • 5 tbsp. low-fat plain yogurt • 1 tsp. flaxseed oil

Juice the pineapple and strawberries. Pour the juice into a blender, add the rest of the ingredients and process until smooth and creamy.

HEALTH BENEFITS
*Flaxseed oil is one of the best vegetarian sources of **omega-3 essential fats**, which are **vital for cellular function** and can increase the body's metabolic rate, helping to **burn excess fat**.*

Nutritional analysis per serving: *Calories 193kcal • Protein 5.2g • Carbohydrates 35.8g [of which sugars 33.9g] • Fat 4.3g*

magic malibu

Packed with vitamin C, especially from the guava and lime, this juice is great for your collagen and elastin production, which are essential for supple, young-looking skin.

1 guava • 1 lime, peeled • 5½oz. pineapple, peeled • scant ⅔ cup coconut milk • ½ papaya, seeded and peeled • a pinch of grated nutmeg • a pinch of cinnamon • ice cubes and grated lime zest, to serve

Juice the guava, lime and pineapple. Pour the juice into a blender, add the rest of the ingredients and process until smooth. Serve over ice and decorate with lime zest.

HEALTH BENEFITS
*Pineapple and papaya are both rich in **digestive enzymes** that encourage digestion and **speed up waste removal** to help keep your **skin clear and fresh**. Coconut milk has **anti-inflammatory properties**, making it a useful ingredient if you suffer from skin rashes.*

Nutritional analysis per serving: *Calories 134kcal • Protein 2.4g • Carbohydrates 30.3g [of which sugars 25.6g] • Fat 1.2g*

< green quencher

Are you suffering with dry skin and hair? Tackle them with this delicious internal moisturizer. Rich in healthy fats, vitamins C and E, and water, this juice helps keep your skin radiant and glowing, and adds a gorgeous luster to your hair.

½ cucumber • 3 kiwifruits, peeled • ½ avocado, peeled and pitted • 1 tbsp. lemon juice • 2 lemon balm leaves • 1 handful of ice cubes

Juice the cucumber and kiwifruits. Pour the juice into a blender, add the rest of the ingredients and process until smooth.

HEALTH BENEFITS
*Lemon balm is a **nerve relaxant and anti-depressant**, so helps **relieve skin breakouts** that are stress related. It also possesses **anti-histamine** properties to help **alleviate inflamed skin**.*

Nutritional analysis per serving: *Calories 200kcal • Protein 4.1g • Carbohydrates 22.7g [of which sugars 20.3g] • Fat 10.8g*

spiced plum warmer

A clear complexion relies on your skin and digestive system moving toxins out of your body. This juice is rich in skin-friendly antioxidants to help combat the onslaught of toxins against your skin, and has plenty of soluble fiber to improve digestion.

2 apples • ½in. piece of gingerroot, peeled • 6 pitted prunes • 2 star anise • 8 cardamon pods

Juice the apples and ginger. Pour the juice into a blender, add ½ cup water and the prunes and process until creamy and thick. Pour into a pan and add the spices, bring to a boil, then reduce the heat to low and simmer gently for 5 minutes. Cool slightly, then strain and serve.

HEALTH BENEFITS
*Cardamon, star anise and ginger are **warming, stimulating** spices that help **improve circulation and soothe digestive problems**, including relieving wind and treating nausea. As digestive aids, they help **cleanse the body**, which is vital to keep your skin glowing.*

Nutritional analysis per serving: *Calories 89kcal • Protein 1.5g • Carbohydrates 21.8g [of which sugars 20.6g] • Fat 0.4g*

persimmon cream

If your hair, eyes and skin are looking a little dull, brighten them up with this protein- and vitamin-packed smoothie. The tofu and soy milk provide phytoestrogens, natural plant hormones that help with PMS and menopausal symptoms, which often affect skin health.

2 persimmons, peeled • 2 apples • 1¾oz. silken tofu • 2¼oz. mango, peeled, pitted and chopped • scant ⅔ cup soy milk

Juice the persimmons and apples. Pour the juice into a blender, add the remaining ingredients and process until creamy.

HEALTH BENEFITS
*Persimmons are **packed with antioxidants** including vitamin C, beta-carotene, lycopene, lutein and zeaxanthin. These are all valuable nutrients for maintaining healthy skin and eyes and for **preventing macular degeneration**. They also provide **soluble fiber,** which **supports waste elimination**, and **manganese**, which your body needs for the production of the enzyme superoxide dismutase, a **powerful antioxidant and liver aid**.*

Nutritional analysis per serving: *Calories 255kcal • Protein 9.5g • Carbohydrates 46.3g [of which sugars 43.3g] • Fat 4.7g*

blemish blitz

This delicious orange juice is packed with beta-carotene, which your body uses to produce vitamin A, an important nutrient in the control of sebum production. Vitamin A is also a powerful anti-aging nutrient and, combined with the zinc from the pumpkin seeds, can help heal and rejuvenate your skin.

½ **sweet potato • 10½oz. cantaloupe melon, peeled • 1 broccoli floret •**
½ **red bell pepper, seeded and cored • 2 tsp. pumpkin seeds**

Juice the vegetables and fruit. Put the juice and pumpkin seeds into a blender and process to combine.

HEALTH BENEFITS
*Pumpkin seeds are a rich source of nutrients essential for healthy skin and hair, including zinc, iron, copper, manganese and protein. They are a good **vegetarian source of omega-3 fats**, which are **anti-inflammatory** and can help **keep your skin looking fresh and glowing**. They also contain plenty of **B-vitamins to lift energy levels**, and **protein to help stabilize blood sugar** and curb cravings.*

Nutritional analysis per serving: *Calories 187kcal • Protein 6.1g • Carbohydrates 30.4g [of which sugars 18.5g] • Fat 5.4g*

balancing act

Give your hair and skin a nourishing boost with this superfood cocktail – a good source of protein, essential fats and phytoestrogens which helps balance hormones and tackle dry, flaky skin to restore a radiant complexion.

5½oz. pineapple, peeled • 2¼oz. baby leaf spinach or collard greens • 1 small banana • 2 tsp. maca root powder • scant ⅔ cup soy milk • 1 tsp. ground flaxseed

Juice the pineapple and spinach. Pour the juice into a blender, add the remaining ingredients and process until creamy.

HEALTH BENEFITS
*Flaxseed is rich in **lignans**, which the body converts into hormone-like substances to help **rebalance hormone levels** and help **prevent hormone-related skin break-outs**, and in **omega-3 fatty acids** to **nourish the body's cells** and keep the skin soft and young looking. Ground flaxseed has a **cleansing effect** on the body.*

Nutritional analysis per serving: *Calories 250kcal • Protein 9.1g • Carbohydrates 43.2g [of which sugars 31.5g] • Fat 5.7g*

instant botox >

If you want to smooth out wrinkles and lines naturally, try this sensational juice, which is packed with skin-nourishing essential fats and hydrating fruits and vegetables to plump up the skin's appearance. It's also bursting with vitamin C to boost your body's production of collagen.

1 apple, plus 1 or 2 extra slices to decorate • 1 orange • ¼ avocado, peeled, pitted and chopped • ½ mango, peeled, pitted and chopped • 1 tbsp. shelled hemp seeds • ½ tsp. agave nectar • 4 tbsp. low-fat plain yogurt • ice cubes, to serve

Juice the apple and orange. Pour the juice into a blender, add all the other ingredients and ⅓ cup water and process until smooth. Serve over ice and decorate with apple slices.

HEALTH BENEFITS
*Plain yogurt is **rich in biotin**, a B-vitamin that helps the **conversion of essential fats into active chemicals for skin-cell health**.*

Nutritional analysis per serving: *Calories 294kcal • Protein 10.5g • Carbohydrates 37.6 [of which sugars 33.5g] • Fat 12.7g*

< blackcurrant burst

Cleansing and rich in vitamin C, this juice is a great healer for any skin complaint and will help keep your complexion smooth and radiant. It is packed with soluble fiber to aid digestion, speeding up the removal of toxins from your body for blemish-free skin.

2 pears • ¾ cup blackcurrants, or blueberries • 1 pink grapefruit, peeled • ice cubes and mint, to serve

Juice all the ingredients. Serve over ice and decorate with a sprig of mint.

HEALTH BENEFITS
*Blackcurrants are power-packed with **vitamin C and bioflavanoids**, which your body needs **for collagen production**. They are also rich in anthocyanidins and polyphenols, **antioxidants** that help **protect against the effects of aging**, as well as **strengthening capillaries** and **tackling inflammation**.*

Nutritional analysis per serving: *Calories 200kcal • Protein 3.2g • Carbohydrates 48.5g [of which sugars 46.2g] • Fat 0.5g*

grape and lemon cleanse

This is a hydrating, cleansing juice to help rejuvenate your skin. Antioxidants in the black grapes can aid capillary function, which can help tackle cellulite or reduce the appearance of prominent veins.

9oz. cantaloupe melon, peeled • 1 lemon, peeled, plus lemon slice to decorate • 1⅓ cups seedless black grapes • ice cubes, to serve

Juice all the ingredients. Serve over ice and decorate with a slice of lemon.

HEALTH BENEFITS
*Black grapes are especially rich in the **flavonoids** quercetin and resveratrol, which have **strong antioxidant and anti-inflammatory properties**. The high water and fiber content of grapes means they are **powerful cleansing foods** that **boost detoxification**.*

Nutritional analysis per serving: *Calories 226kcal • Protein 2.8g • Carbohydrates 55.9g [of which sugars 53.2g] • Fat 0.6g*

power juices

If you often wake up in the morning feeling unrefreshed, or if you find it hard to stay alert during the day, the vitality-boosting juices in this chapter are for you. Every one of them is packed with the nutrients your body needs to generate energy: the juices are low in refined carbohydrates and rich in protein, and will optimize your mental and physical efficiency all day, every day. Some of the juices and shakes, such as Tofu Power Cream, are intended to kickstart your body into action; while others, such as the Highland Boost, provide instant zest from natural sugars, but also offer slow-releasing energy from oats and nuts to keep you on an even keel from morning to night; still others are power-packed exercise shakes that will help restore your energy after a workout. All in all, this chapter bursts with power juices to crank up your vitality. And with a sample energy program to follow, too, it couldn't be easier or more delicious to put the spring back into your step.

◁ green power, page 130

the power juice program

Your body is constantly using oxygen to convert fuel, in the form of the carbohydrates, fats and protein in your food, into energy, in a cycle known as the Krebs cycle. In order for this cycle to work efficiently, your body needs certain vitamins and minerals that support the process.

Low levels of these vital nutrients impair the Krebs cycle and leave you feeling tired and lethargic. Your energy levels are also affected by how sugary or processed is the food that you eat. Candy and highly refined, white-flour foods cause rapid fluctuations in your blood-sugar levels, resulting in a crash in energy that leaves you feeling tired and lethargic, as well as affecting your mood and your ability to concentrate. To supply your body with sustainable energy, it's important to focus on eating not only foods that provide the nutrients you need to produce energy, but also foods that release sugar slowly into your bloodstream.

Power juice nutrients All the power juices in this chapter have been put together to provide high-energy nutrients. So, if you eat a diet that is rich in healthy fats, high-quality protein (for example, from lean poultry and fish) and complex carbohydrates, which are found in wholegrain foods, fruits and vegetables, and intersperse your meals with juices from this chapter, you'll be giving your body all it needs to feel fully energized throughout the day.

Many of the juices are packed with protein, which is essential for stabilizing your blood-sugar levels to prevent the highs and lows of the energy rollercoaster. Protein is also vital for muscle building and to support your body's recovery and repair after exercise – and exercise is essential in any weight loss program.

In addition, the juices in this chapter provide the vital nutrients your body needs to support the Krebs cycle, including B-vitamins, vitamin C, magnesium and chromium.

Using the power juices If you've been feeling particularly low in energy for a while, try to drink two or three of the power juices every day for a month; otherwise try to drink one daily as part of your usual healthy-eating routine. In the box below, I've given a sample meal plan to help you get started on a dedicated energy-boost program. The plan is designed to improve both your mental and your physical energy by supplying you with foods that balance your blood sugar and optimize your alertness. Stabilizing your blood sugar will keep you fuller for longer, avoiding energy dips that can leave you tired and mentally drained.

It's also really important that, while you're trying to get your energy levels back on track (and as much as you can generally), you avoid processed, white, refined foods, such as white bread and pasta, and sweets and cakes.

power juice plan sample day

Breakfast Green Power **(page 130)**. Oatmeal with reduced-fat milk, with blueberries and sliced almonds

Mid-morning snack Oat cakes spread with cottage cheese

Lunch Highland Boost **(page 138)**. Vegetable and bean soup (for two): Chop 1 red onion, 2 garlic cloves, 2 celery sticks and 2 carrots and sauté in a pan in 1 tsp. olive oil for 2–3 minutes. Add 3½ cups vegetable stock; season. Bring to a boil, reduce the heat to low, cover and simmer for 20 minutes until soft. Add 14oz. drained, canned mixed beans and a splash balsamic vinegar. Heat through. Sprinkle with hemp seeds. Serve with 1 wholewheat pita

Mid-afternoon snack Chocolate Sesame Cream **(page 142)**

Dinner Grilled lamb steak with steamed colorful vegetables (such as broccoli, carrots and red cabbage) and a small baked potato. Bowl of cherries

green power

This green juice provides an amazing array of enzymes, vitamins, minerals and amino acids that your body can rapidly absorb for an instant energy kick. Packed with revitalizing chlorophyll, Green Power is true liquid vitality.

½ cucumber • 1 apple • 5½oz. pineapple, peeled • 1 large handful of kale leaves • 1 handful of sprouts, plus extra to decorate, or 1 tsp. wheatgrass powder • 2 tsp. sunflower seeds

Juice all the ingredients except the seeds. Pour the juice into a blender, add the seeds and process until smooth. Pour and decorate with a few sprouts.

HEALTH BENEFITS
*Sunflower seeds are a concentrated source of nutrients, particularly **health-boosting vitamin E, selenium and magnesium**. The antioxidants vitamin E and selenium have **anti-inflammatory properties** useful for **joint health**. The seeds also contain **beneficial unsaturated fats and phytosterols** to help lower cholesterol and **support heart health**.*

Nutritional analysis per serving: *Calories 184kcal • Protein 5.7g • Carbohydrates 28g [of which sugars 24.7g] • Fat 6.1g*

tofu power cream >

Sweet and creamy, this is a delicious, thick smoothie that's perfect for a quick, satisfying breakfast. Rich in vitamin C and beta-carotene, as well as plenty of natural sugars, it will give you a quick lift whenever you wake up feeling fatigued.

3 oranges, peeled • 2½oz. silken tofu • 4 dried soft apricots • 1 peach, pitted, plus extra slice to decorate • scant ²/₃ cup soy milk

Juice the oranges, then pour the juice into a blender, add the rest of the ingredients and process until smooth. Pour into a glass and decorate with a peach slice.

HEALTH BENEFITS
*Dried apricots are a concentrated source of nutrients and natural sugars, including **beta-carotene, iron, potassium, calcium and magnesium**. Hemoglobin, the protein that carries oxygen around your body, needs iron to function properly, so iron is an essential nutrient **for good energy levels**.*

Nutritional analysis per serving: *Calories 266kcal • Protein 14.7g • Carbohydrates 40.8g [of which sugars 38.2g] • Fat 6g*

< pear cashew magic

Spinach and cashews make this an iron-rich shake that is pure power in a glass. Pears and lemon offer plenty of vitamin C to help your body turn nutrients into energy.

1½ pears, peeled • ½ lemon, peeled • 1 celery stick, plus 2 extra to decorate • 1 small handful of spinach leaves • ¼ cup cashews

Juice the fruit and vegetables. Pour the juice into a blender, add the cashews and ½ cup water and process until creamy. Pour and decorate with celery sticks.

HEALTH BENEFITS
*Cashews are rich in **copper and iron**, both important nutrients for **building red blood cells**. They also provide **protein, magnesium and zinc** for **healthy bones, hair and skin**.*

Nutritional analysis per serving: *Calories 317kcal • Protein 8.5g • Carbohydrates 30.5g [of which sugars 24.2g] • Fat 18.7g*

satay smoothie

This smoothie combines protein and natural sugars for both instant and slower-release energy, to sustain you thoughout the day. The cucumber, celery and watermelon are great hydrating foods that refresh and rejuvenate your body.

8oz. watermelon • 1 tomato • 1 celery stick • ½ cucumber • 1 tsp. sugar- and salt-free smooth peanut butter

Juice the fruit and vegetables. Pour the juice into a blender, add the peanut butter and process until creamy.

HEALTH BENEFITS
*This combination of vegetables and fruit supplies plenty of **potassium and other electrolytes** to help **maintain fluid balance**, which is particularly important following a workout.*

Nutritional analysis per serving: *Calories 146kcal • Protein 4.6g • Carbohydrates 21.6g [of which sugars 19.9g] • Fat 5.2g*

< blood booster

Whenever you're feeling a little run down or low in energy, reach for this purple tonic. The beet and spinach are great ingredients for boosting oxygen-carrying hemoglobin in your blood, while the cucumber hydrates your body, helping to relieve fatigue and restore electrolyte balance, which is essential for maintaining energy levels and muscle function.

½ cucumber • 1 beet • 1 handful of spinach leaves • 2 apples • 1 tsp. brewer's yeast or nutritional yeast flakes

Juice the vegetables and fruit. Pour the juice into a blender, add the brewer's yeast and process to combine.

HEALTH BENEFITS
*Brewer's yeast is an inactive yeast **rich in B-vitamins, amino acids and minerals**. Because of its high B-vitamin content it is a great energy booster for between meals and **supports the body's metabolism**, making it easier to **control your weight**.*

Nutritional analysis per serving: *Calories 108kcal • Protein 4g • Carbohydrates 22.2g [of which sugars 20.7g] • Fat 0.8g*

the invigorator

This enlivening juice is a perfect pick-me-up. Beet is a superb blood tonic, helping to increase the oxygen-carrying capacity of your blood and boosting your circulation. The addition of nori flakes provides a great source of trace minerals and iodine to kickstart your metabolism and support the health of your thyroid gland, which regulates the speed at which your body burns energy.

½ beet • ½ carrot • 1 apple • 1 orange, peeled • ¼ cucumber • ½ tsp. flaxseed oil or omega 3-6-9 oil • ½ tsp. nori flakes

Juice the vegetables and fruit. Stir in the oil and nori flakes.

HEALTH BENEFITS
*Nori is rich in the **antioxidant vitamins A and C**, and **vitamin B2** and the mineral **magnesium**, which are essential **for energy production**. Flaxseed oil is rich in **omega-3 essential fats**, which the body uses to produce hormone-like substances known as prostaglandins, which in turn **control metabolism and reduce inflammation**. These healthy fats help you burn fat and **reduce the levels of cholesterol and triglycerides** (fats) in your blood.*

Nutritional analysis per serving: *Calories 115kcal • Protein 3.3g • Carbohydrates 23.9g [of which sugars 21.7g] • Fat 1.4g*

hemp and greens

Packed with energizing essential fats and protein, this smoothie is sweet and satisfying. It makes a perfect pre-sports drink or post-recovery snack to keep hunger pangs at bay. Make up a batch and sip it through the day, or drink it for breakfast when time is tight.

½ banana • 2 large handfuls of spinach leaves • scant ⅔ cup coconut water • ½ mango, peeled, pitted and chopped • 1 tbsp. shelled hemp seeds • 1 tbsp. agave nectar • ½ tsp. cinnamon • ice cubes, to serve

Process all the ingredients in a blender until smooth. Serve over ice.

HEALTH BENEFITS
*Hemp seeds are loaded with **omega-6 and omega-3 essential fatty acids** that boost the **health of your body's cells**. They are also a great **source of protein**. Rich in fats and antioxidants, they are great for **countering inflammation** in the body as a result of ill health or injury.*

Nutritional analysis per serving: *Calories 265kcal • Protein 8.2g • Carbohydrates 43.5g [of which sugars 31.8g] • Fat 7.8g*

sweet squash >

Forget mass-market, sugary energy drinks, this juice is packed with energizing antioxidants, vitamin C and beta-carotene, and contains plenty of protein and healthy fats for a sustaining energy fix. For a fizzy option, leave out the water and top with sparkling water instead.

2 oranges, peeled • 5½oz. butternut squash, peeled and seeded • 2 tbsp. pecans • 2 dates • ½ tsp. vanilla extract

Juice the oranges and butternut squash. Pour the juice into a blender, add the remaining ingredients and scant ⅔ cup water and process until creamy.

HEALTH BENEFITS
*Butternut squash provides superb levels of beta-carotene, lutein and zeaxanthin, **powerful antioxidants** that promote **eye health** and have **anti-inflammatory properties** that make them useful for joint conditions, including **rheumatoid arthritis**. A good source of **soluble fiber**, squash is beneficial for **digestive health** and can help **reduce the risk of bowel cancer**.*

Nutritional analysis per serving: *Calories 259kcal • Protein 5.8g • Carbohydrates 36.8g [of which sugars 29.5g] • Fat 10.9g*

highland boost

The oat flakes and nuts in this healthy version of a Scottich cranachan (a dessert made with whipped cream, raspberries and whisky) provide plenty of slow-releasing energy, as well as protein to reduce hunger pangs (if you want to keep the smoothie gluten-free, use buckwheat flakes instead). Hazelnuts in particular are a good source of protein, and they are also rich in the mineral manganese, which stabilizes blood sugar.

½ tsp. coconut butter or olive oil • ½ tsp. agave nectar or Manuka or raw honey • ¼ tsp. cinnamon • 1½ tbsp. oat flakes • 1 tbsp. hazelnuts • 2 plums • 1 cup frozen raspberries • ½ tsp. rosewater • 4 tbsp. low-fat plain yogurt

Heat the coconut butter, agave and cinnamon in a pan. Stir in the oat flakes and hazelnuts. Toast for 2–3 minutes until slightly golden, then set aside. Juice the plums. Pour the juice into a blender, add the remaining ingredients and the oat mixture and process until creamy and smooth. Dilute with a little water if too thick.

HEALTH BENEFITS
*Hazelnuts are one of the richest sources of **vitamin E**, a powerful antioxidant that helps **neutralize free radicals** that can damage cells leading to ill health. The raspberries and plums provide **fiber to aid bowel health**, and are packed with antioxidants, vitamins and minerals for general well-being. Manuka honey is **antiviral, antibacterial and wound-healing**, and helps to **maintain a healthy digestive system**.*

Nutritional analysis per serving: *Calories 314kcal • Protein 11.3g • Carbohydrates 38.4g [of which sugars 16.8g] • Fat 14.2g*

pear energizer

For a quick boost when you feel your energy levels are flagging, try this refreshing juice packed with hydrating water and sweet, natural sugars. It makes a perfect pre-workout drink.

2 pears • ¾ cup green grapes • 1 yellow plum, pitted • 3 mint leaves • 1 tsp. flaxseed oil • sparkling water, to serve

Juice the pears, grapes, plum and mint leaves. Stir the oil into the juice and top with sparkling water.

HEALTH BENEFITS

*Pears contain **high levels of dietary fiber** to help keep the bowels in good health, and may help **reduce the risk of colon cancer**. They are also rich in **immunity-boosting vitamin C** and in the **mineral copper**, which has an **antioxidant** effect on the body. Green grapes have a rich mineral content that helps **rebalance the body's acid–alkali levels** and **restore electrolytes**, which enable your cells to communicate with one another and can become depleted during exercise. They are also great for **cleansing the liver and kidneys**.*

Nutritional analysis per serving: *Calories 248kcal • Protein 2.7g • Carbohydrates 57.4g [of which sugars 53.1g] • Fat 2.6g*

black fig delight

Bursting with natural sugars, grapes are a perfect energy fuel and provide essential minerals that can be lost during an intensive workout. Adding a scoop of protein powder helps stabilize blood-sugar levels to keep your muscles fuelled for longer.

heaping 1 cup seedless black grapes • 1 apple • 3 figs • 3 kumquats, pitted • 3 tbsp. blueberries • 1½ tbsp. vanilla whey protein powder • ice cubes, to serve

Juice the grapes, apple, figs and kumquats. Pour the juice into a blender and add the blueberries and protein powder. Process until smooth. Serve over ice.

HEALTH BENEFITS
*Kumquats provide plenty of **vitamin C to support the Krebs cycle** (see page 128), and by juicing the whole fruit, you also extract **beneficial bioflavonoids** found in the pith, under the rind. These potent antioxidants have been shown to **protect against some forms of cancer.***

Nutritional analysis per serving: *Calories*

athlete's shake >

Easily digested and nourishing, this superb smoothie makes a perfect pre- or post-workout snack to boost energy levels and build up muscle stamina. You don't have to be an athlete to benefit from it, though – it's also a great one to try if you're feeling under the weather or recovering from an illness.

8oz. cherries, pitted • 2 pomegranates, seeds and flesh • 1½ tbsp. vanilla whey protein powder • scant ²/₃ cup coconut milk • 1 tsp. almond butter • 1 tsp. lecithin granules

Juice the cherries and pomegranates. Pour the juice into a blender, add the rest of the ingredients and process until smooth and creamy.

HEALTH BENEFITS
*Whey is an excellent choice for athletes or anyone on the go, since it provides a **balanced source of amino acids** to help **prevent muscle breakdown**. It is also a fantastic source of calcium (for **bone strength**) and has **anti-inflammatory** properties.*

Nutritional analysis per serving: *Calories 331kcal • Protein 25.6g • Carbohydrates 47.4g [of which sugars 43.4g] • Fat 5.5g*

chocolate sesame cream

Creamy and filling, this protein-packed smoothie will not only satisfy your chocolate cravings, but also provide instant energy to replenish your stocks of glycogen, the molecule that stores energy in your muscles, when you're feeling physically fatigued.

½ cup skim milk • scant ½ cup low-fat plain yogurt • 1 small banana • 2 prunes, pitted • ¼ tsp. cinnamon • a pinch of grated nutmeg • 1 tbsp. raw cacao powder • 1 tsp. tahini

Process all the ingredients in a blender until thick and creamy.

HEALTH BENEFITS
*Rich in phytosterols, sesame seeds (which are used to make tahini) can help **lower cholesterol** and **boost your immune system**. They are also packed with **calcium and magnesium** to **nourish your bones and muscles**, and **protein and essential fats** to help **balance blood-sugar levels**.*

Nutritional analysis per serving: *Calories 279kcal • Protein 13.8g • Carbohydrates 44.9g [of which sugars 31.2g] • Fat 5.8g*

energy kick

This comforting, milky drink bursts with superfoods to put the spring back in your step. It is an excellent source of protein and can help stabilize blood sugar and keep energy levels high.

generous 1 cup almond milk • 2 tbsp. raw cacao powder • 1 tsp. maca root powder • 1 tbsp. agave nectar • 1 tsp. flaxseed oil • ½ tsp. powdered ginseng or a few drops ginseng tincture (optional)

Process all the ingredients in a blender until smooth and creamy.

HEALTH BENEFITS
*Popular with athletes to give a natural energy boost, ginseng can **build muscle and endurance**. A well-known **adaptogen**, it can be useful to help the body **tackle stress and address any hormone imbalances**. It is also rich in a wide range of vitamins, minerals and amino acids, including **energy-boosting B-vitamins and iron**.*

Nutritional analysis per serving: *Calories 289kcal • Protein 9.1g • Carbohydrates 48.1g [of which sugars 10.9g] • Fat 7.5g*

immunity juices

If you're healthy and your body is well nourished, your immune system is much more able to fight off infections. However, any diet that lacks essential immunity-supporting nutrients can make you prone to illness. In this chapter you'll find a range of immunity juices that can help reduce the chances of you getting ill, and can help you get better quickly if you do get sick. All the juices burst with the antioxidants, vitamins and minerals we know optimize immune function, helping your body manufacture disease-fighting white blood cells and antibodies. So, for an antioxidant boost to fight off free radicals, why not start the day with a tropical Passion Coconut Cream or a shot of Green Tropical Burst? If you're already feeling below par or are fighting off a cold, grab a glass of Berry Healer or the sensational Honey and Grapefruit Sour. These, and all the other delicious juices in this chapter, are packed with superfoods so that you can literally drink yourself to a stronger, healthier body.

< citrus ginger tea, page 150

the immunity juice program

Your incredibly complex immune system involves various mechanisms that help your body tackle invaders, such as viruses, bacteria and fungi, that make you ill. It is essential to your short- and long-term well-being.

Fighting night and day to overcome much more than coughs, colds and flu, a well-functioning immune system protects you against immune-related diseases such as cancer, prevents autoimmune conditions such as rheumatoid arthritis, and helps to heal injury.

Given its non-stop work, your immunity relies upon a steady supply of vital nutrients for its function. Many of the juices in this chapter include protein foods, such as nuts, seeds, dairy and tofu, which help your body manufacture new immune cells to regenerate and renew its healing abilities. Protein foods will also help you convalesce, since they help your body rebuild and restore itself back to health.

Immunity-boosting nutrients You'll find that all the immunity juices are rich in protective antioxidants, particularly vitamins A, C and E, and carotenoids, bioflavonoids, selenium and zinc. These help your body reduce inflammation and produce specialist immunity cells, and they support your body's antibody production. Juices that are rich in vitamin B6 help your body produce amino acids that are vital to immune function.

Probiotic foods, such as yogurt and buttermilk, can help stimulate immune function in your gut, so there are plenty of juices that include these, too. Some of the immunity juices include specific antimicrobial foods and herbs, such as Manuka honey, garlic, onion and echinacea, which can help ward off infections, coughs and colds.

Using the immunity juices If you're suffering from a particular condition, or have suffered repeated colds in the last few months, I recommend you drink two or three immunity juices every day for a month to help rebuild your immune system. Use the immunity juice sample day (below) to get you started on an immunity-strengthening program. Try to keep your diet low in sugar, too, since sugar is a great enemy of your immune system. Going forward, one immunity juice daily should help keep your immune system functioning at optimum levels.

immunity juice plan sample day

Breakfast Cherry Buttermilk Smoothie **(page 156)**. Poached egg on wholewheat toast spread with tahini

Mid-morning snack 1 handful of Brazil nuts and 1 handful of prunes

Lunch Vegetable Tonic **(page 155)**. Baked organic chicken breast served with salad of: 1 chopped cooked beet, 1 chopped tomato and chopped ½ red bell pepper, all combined with 1 handful of dark salad greens. Sprinkle the salad with pumpkin seeds and dress with a little lemon juice. Mixed berries with low-fat plain yogurt

Mid-afternoon snack Citrus Ginger Tea **(page 150)**. Oatcakes spread with nut butter

Dinner Bowl of Miso soup (use a good-quality brand and follow the package instructions). Stir-fried shrimp and mixed vegetables: Mix together 1 tbsp. each of lemon juice and soy sauce with ½ tsp. grated ginger and 1 chopped garlic clove. Heat a little olive oil in a wok or frying pan and add a bag of mixed stir-fry vegetables (about 5½oz.) with the lemon juice mixture and cook over high heat until crisp. Add 3½oz. cooked shrimp and heat through. Season well and top with fresh cilantro leaves. Accompany with ½ cup cooked brown Basmati rice (about ¼ cup uncooked).

< passion coconut cream

Orange, passion fruit and guava – this smoothie is packed with vitamin C to help you fight off colds and flu, and so much more.

1 guava, peeled • 1 orange, peeled • 4 passion fruit, pulp and seeds • scant ²/₃ cup coconut milk

Juice the guava and orange. Pour the juice into a blender, add the rest of the ingredients and process until creamy.

HEALTH BENEFITS
*As well as loads of vitamin C, passion fruits provide plenty of **phytochemicals, phenolic acids and flavonoids**, which are all known for their **antimicrobial properties** and their ability to **inhibit the growth of cancer cells**. Coconut milk is rich in **lauric acid**, which the body converts into an **antiviral and antibacterial** substance known as monolaurin.*

Nutritional analysis per serving: *Calories 115kcal • Protein 3.8g • Carbohydrates 24g [of which sugars 22.8g] • Fat 1.1g*

pecan pie

Fruity and creamy, this juice is an immunity-boosting sensation that's packed with antioxidants. The protein from the nuts helps boost your body's levels of infection-fighting white blood cells.

3½oz. sweet potato • 1 apple • ½ banana • 1 tsp. Manuka honey • 2 tbsp. pecans • ½ tsp. cinnamon • ½ tsp. pumpkin pie spice

Juice the sweet potato and apple. Pour the juice into a blender, add the remaining ingredients and scant 1 cup water and process until smooth.

HEALTH BENEFITS
*Pecans provide **good amounts of ellagic acid**, which is thought to have **anti-cancer properties**, as well as the antioxidant nutrients **vitamin E and selenium**. Manuka honey is well known for its **antimicrobial and antiviral properties**, while sweet potato is rich in the **antioxidant vitamin A**.*

Nutritional analysis per serving: *Calories 284kcal • Protein 3.5g • Carbohydrates 45.5g [of which sugars 27.2g] • Fat 11.1g*

citrus ginger tea

The combination of citrus, honey and green tea in this juice makes it a super-protective drink that's perfect for when you're feeling below par. The spices make it wonderfully warming, to help nurture you back to your feet.

1 green tea bag • 1 cinnamon stick • 1 tsp. Manuka honey • 1 pink grapefruit, peeled • 1 orange, peeled, plus extra slice to decorate • 1 lemon, peeled • ½in. piece of gingerroot, peeled • ice cubes, to serve (optional)

Place the tea bag and cinnamon stick in a pitcher and pour over scant ⅔ cup boiling water. Stir in the honey, allow to steep for 5 minutes, then strain. Juice the remaining ingredients and stir the juice into the tea. Pour and drink immediately, with a slice of orange to decorate, or cool and serve over ice.

HEALTH BENEFITS
*This drink is rich in **antioxidants and bioflavonoids** to help **reduce the risk of certain cancers**, and in **vitamin C** to help increase your body's **antibody production**. Manuka honey has **antiseptic and antimicrobial** properties, and is well known for its ability to **treat burns, ulcers, wounds and a wide range of infections**.*

Nutritional analysis per serving: *Calories 125kcal • Protein 3.3g • Carbohydrates 28.7g [of which sugar 27.2g] • Fat 0.5g*

vanilla shake

This sweet, tropical-tasting smoothie is rich in protein, an essential nutrient for your body's defenses. Yogurt is a useful source of beneficial bacteria that can help support your overall immune health by keeping in check the "bad" bacteria in your gut.

10 lychees, pitted • 1½ tbsp. vanilla whey protein powder • 1 small banana • 2 Brazil nuts • scant ²/₃ cup low-fat vanilla or plain yogurt

Process all the ingredients in a blender until smooth. Dilute with a little water if too thick.

HEALTH BENEFITS
Brazil nuts are an excellent source of **selenium,** *which your body needs to produce the antioxidant glutathione, which in turn helps* **protect your body from oxidative stress and cancerous cells.**

Nutritional analysis per serving: *Calories 378kcal • Protein 30.4g • Carbohydrates 52.8g [of which sugars 47.2g] • Fat 6.5g*

berry healer

Delicious warm, this is a perfect winter juice. Echinacea tincture is an herbal extract that has been shown to boost immune function and help protect against the cold virus. Together with Manuka honey, echinacea supercharges the protective power of this juice.

2 apples • ¾ cup blueberries • ¾ cup blackcurrants, or blueberries • 15 drops echinacea tincture • 1 tsp. Manuka honey

Juice the fruit, then stir in the tincture and honey. Warm in a stainless steel pan to serve, if desired.

HEALTH BENEFITS
*The combination of berries in this juice provides an amazing range of **antioxidants**, particularly bioflavanoids, anthocyanidins and vitamin C, to **nourish immune cells and antibody production**. These antioxidants also help trigger aspects of your body's **fight against carcinogens**, helping to protect against certain cancers.*

Nutritional analysis per serving: *Calories 153kcal • Protein 2.3g • Carbohydrates 37.4g [of which sugars 35.7g] • Fat 0.4g*

honeyed figs >

If you've been recovering from an illness, have had a poor appetite, or are in need of a quick pick-me-up, this is the perfect juice to give you an extra boost back into health.

3 figs • 2 apples • scant ⅔ cup low-fat plain yogurt • ½ tsp. cinnamon, plus extra for dusting • 1 tsp. Manuka honey • 1 tbsp. toasted sliced almonds

Juice the figs and apples. Put the juice and the remaining ingredients into a blender and process until smooth. Serve dusted with a little cinnamon.

HEALTH BENEFITS
*Figs contain compounds that have **anti-cancer properties**. They are also a rich source of **natural sugars, iron and potassium**, which provide instant energy and help **restore fluid balance**. Great for digestive upsets, figs contain ficin, an enzyme that **helps soothe the gut**.*

Nutritional analysis per serving: *Calories 288kcal • Protein 11.8g • Carbohydrates 39.9g [of which sugars 37.6g] • Fat 10.2g*

< cranberry syrup

Much better for you than a sugary cough mixture, try this delicious pink nectar to tackle coughs, colds and sore throats. Cranberries can help boost the body's resistance to viral, bacterial and fungal attack.

2¼ cups cranberries • 1 orange, peeled • 1 tsp. Manuka honey • 1 cup raspberries

Juice the cranberries and orange. Pour the juice into a blender, add the honey and raspberries and process until smooth.

HEALTH BENEFITS
*Cranberries are packed with compounds known as **anthocyanidins**, which are thought to have **antioxidant and wound-healing properties**. These berries are well known for **keeping the urinary tract healthy**, but have also been shown to help **inhibit cancerous cells**, tackle **coughs and sore throats** and prevent **gastrointestinal infections**.*

Nutritional analysis per serving: *Calories 130kcal• Protein 3.9g • Carbohydrates 29.3g [of which sugars 27.9g]• Fat 0.7g*

vegetable tonic

Packed with protective antioxidants, this savory combination makes a delicious – and healthier – alternative to the tomato or vegetable juices that you can buy in the stores.

2 celery sticks • 1 small garlic clove • 4 tomatoes • 1 large handful of spinach and watercress leaves • 2 carrots

Juice all the ingredients and mix well.

HEALTH BENEFITS
*Watercress and spinach provide **iron and vitamin C for energy and stamina**, while the medley of veggies is packed full of protective beta-carotene, lycopene, lutein and zeaxanthin to help **prevent age-related macular degeneration** and other chronic conditions. Garlic contains **powerful detoxifying and immune-boosting sulfurous compounds**, including allicin, which is thought to help **prevent the growth of cancer cells**. A **powerful antibiotic**, garlic helps **clear infections**, especially in the digestive tract, and is an effective **decongestant**, useful in the **relief of cold and cough symptoms**.*

Nutritional analysis per serving: *Calories 107kcal• Protein 5g • Carbohydrates 18.7g [of which sugars 17.1g]• Fat 1.9g*

cherry buttermilk smoothie

This rosy-colored shake is healing and rejuvenating. Buttermilk is useful if you are lactose-sensitive, because its beneficial live cultures convert lactose into more digestible lactic acid. If you can't find buttermilk, use low-fat plain yogurt instead.

2 apples • ½ cup buttermilk • 4oz. cherries, pitted • 1 small banana

Juice the apples. Pour the juice into a blender, add the remaining ingredients and process until smooth. Dilute with a little water if too thick.

HEALTH BENEFITS
*Like yogurt, buttermilk contains plenty of **beneficial bacteria** to help support immune health in the gut. Cherries are well known to help **relieve aching bones and joints** and are rich in **flavonoids**, which protect **against certain cancers**. Drunk regularly, this shake may help **ease tummy upsets and diarrhea**.*

Nutritional analysis per serving: *Calories 240kcal • Protein 6.8g • Carbohydrates 53.8g [of which sugars 49.5g] • Fat 1.1g*

green tropical burst >

Light and refreshing, this green juice is great to speed recovery. The coconut water helps restore the body's fluid levels, which can become unbalanced during times of illness.

1 pear • 5½oz. broccoli florets, plus extra stem to decorate • 1 handful of wheatgrass or 1 tsp. wheatgrass powder • scant 2/3 cup coconut water • 6 lychees, pitted

Juice the pear and broccoli, and the fresh wheatgrass, if using. Pour the juice into a blender, add the remaining ingredients (including the wheatgrass powder, if using) and process until smooth. Serve decorated with a broccoli stem.

HEALTH BENEFITS
*Wheatgrass is **rich in chlorophyll**, which is similar in composition to human blood and **oxygenates your cells**, and **vitamins B, C, E and carotene**, which **destroy free radicals**. It is also packed with **amino acids that aid cell regeneration**. Broccoli contains **sulfurous compounds** that help **protect the liver**.*

Nutritional analysis per serving: *Calories 190kcal • Protein 7.9g • Carbohydrates 37.3g [of which sugars 28.7g] • Fat 1.6g*

< sunset booster

If you've been pushing yourself hard, this dreamy juice offers red fruits to give your immune system a boost and keep illness at bay, as well as banana to restore your stamina and energy.

2 tamarillos • 1 pink grapefruit, peeled • 6oz. strawberries • 1 small banana

Juice the tamarillos, grapefruit and strawberries. Pour the juice into a blender, add the banana and process until smooth.

HEALTH BENEFITS
*Tamarillos contain the **antioxidant vitamins A, C and E**, as well as **fatigue-fighting iron and potassium**. Low in calories and a **good source of fiber**, they can help **stabilize blood-sugar levels** and **support digestive health**.*

Nutritional analysis per serving: *Calories 194kcal • Protein 5.2g • Carbohydrates 43.7g [of which sugars 39.9g] • Fat 0.8g*

honey and grapefruit sour

If you have a sore throat or a winter flu, savor this comforting, nourishing drink, designed to soothe and heal.

1 grapefruit, peeled • ½in. piece of gingerroot, peeled • 9oz. pineapple, peeled • 4 cloves • 1 tsp. Manuka honey

Juice the grapefruit, ginger and pineapple. Pour the juice into a pan, add the cloves and honey and warm gently over low heat. Remove from the heat and allow to infuse for 5 minutes, then strain and drink.

HEALTH BENEFITS
*Naturally **antibacterial and anti-inflammatory**, cloves offer effective **relief for aching teeth and sore throats**. The essential oil in cloves contains a compound called **eugenol**, which is useful for **tackling bacterial infection and inflammation**.*

Nutritional analysis per serving: *Calories 175kcal • Protein 2.5g • Carbohydrates 42.4g [of which sugars 40.3g] • Fat 1.1g*

index